Sana Teaching Painting and Drawing
(applying the simplest technique) Volume 2

Author : mohammad manochehri

Cover by : maryam alsadat anjam

ISBN : 978-1939123954

Publisher : Supreme Century

No. of Pages : 108

@Sana1art

WWW.ART-SANA.COM

Awards :
5 Gold
Trophies from the National Congress of the Elders of Skill and Education And from the National Congress of the bests of Iran

Introduction
Hello to the honorable audience

The present work is the second volume of Sana Drawing and Painting Teaching "applying the simplest method" whose first volume has been remarkably appreciated. The work is the matching sequence of the former one. We hope it will be useful to improve its audience's general and artistic talents. In this book, we have concentrated on step- by- step method of drawing and painting with colorful pencils (in a way which makes possible for every art student to follow it). We have also tried to use various patterns and subjects. Hopefully, it is useful and practical to cause innovation and artistic skills. It is necessary to mention that in the book we have avoided theories as much as possible and focused instead on teaching the art through visually analyzing the step by step creation of a painting. To take the most advantage of the book, it is necessary to provide the first volume of the series which is helpful to make us familiar with the basics of the art, applying a simplified language. The exercises in that book also help us to get ready and more skillful for the second volume.

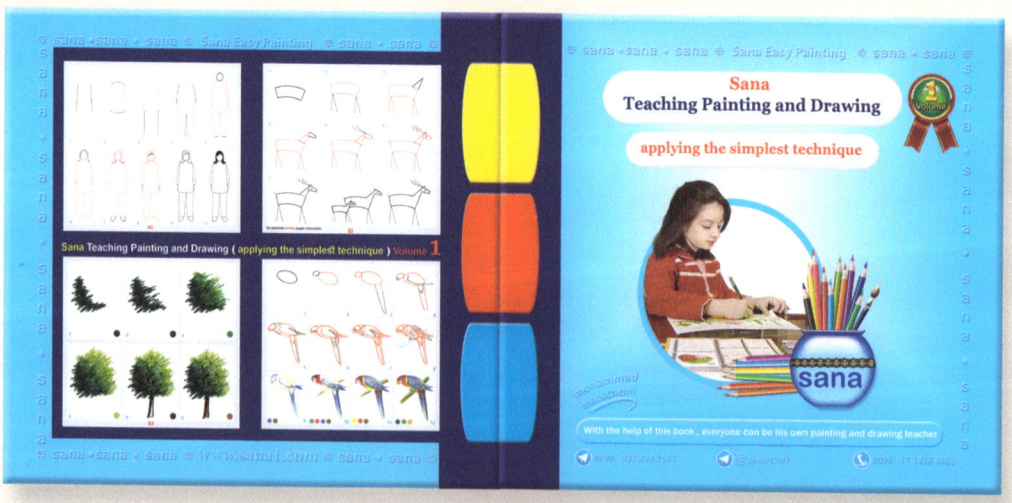

The pictures on the cover of the first volume of the book series which is recommended to be provided and practiced before going to the next volume (as the basics of visual arts have been briefly described in the book) .

A word for teachers and parents

With all due respects to all, due to lack of professional art teachers in elementary schools of Iran the skill of drawing and painting has yet to reach a reasonable standard amongst the students.
To increase the standard the teachers need to be trained. In this book we have taken steps to simplify the training of this basic and necessary field, especially for children and teenagers. The products are named SANA and the method used is the result of years of experience and teaching in different school levels and is presented as a codified method. This package and method not only focuses on teaching and creating drawing and painting skills and beautiful handwriting in children and teenagers but also provides means of growth and development of their other skills.

The purpose of SANA

1) The teachers can teach and instruct the students at a professional level in drawing, painting, collage and beautiful handwriting without having any experience in them.
2) The SANA package is designed to stimulate the minds of student thereby increasing their interest in drawing.
3) By this unique method, a close relationship is established between the hand and the brain of the student.
4) SANA teaches the students that they should have a goal in their minds and analyze that goal and then reach that target with a proper and principled.
5) SANA establishes order and discipline and helps increase focus in the students.
6) SANA will increase self-confidence and self-belief of the student.

SANA can be used to teach drawings and paintings to teenagers.

1) Free Drawing and Painting.   2) Teaching.   3) Creativity.

SANA is focusing on the second item which is teaching. Although the teacher maybe aware of the knowledge and experience, but we shall introduce the methods briefly.

1) Free Drawing and Painting

In this step the student has the liberty to use his/her imagination and personal taste to draw and paint and describe his/her art . The student uses his/her emotional feelings and imagination along his/her skills to create an artifact . Therefore to complete this step , he/she needs to explain and describe his/her art to the audience .

2) Teaching

This step focuses on teaching and developing of Drawing and Painting practically and theoretically .
The teaching has made the job easy for the teachers .

3) Creativity

The purpose of this step is developing imagination, innovation and focus of the students . This can be achieved through various ways . For example , we can draw a small object like an eye and request the students to complete it or we can narrate a story or a historical event and ask them to illustrate it . We may also draw a part of a painting and ask the students to complete the painting .

All the best !

@sana1397

WWW.ART-SANA.COM

Nature and landscape : Since old days, nature has always been a subject of interest for the artists, there are few important principles which have been taken into notice respecting perspective and it's primary and main principles :

1) - In nature, consider the horizon which is the line between the sky and earth.

2) - Considering the facts that distant things are smaller, their color fade and they seem blur and as they get closer, they become bigger, more clear and colors are richer (in order to have a more natural looking painting we should follow the above points).

Keep in mind if you want to show the texture using the coloring pencils, you should use the pencil in a certain way
(Page 42, Vol 1 of this book)

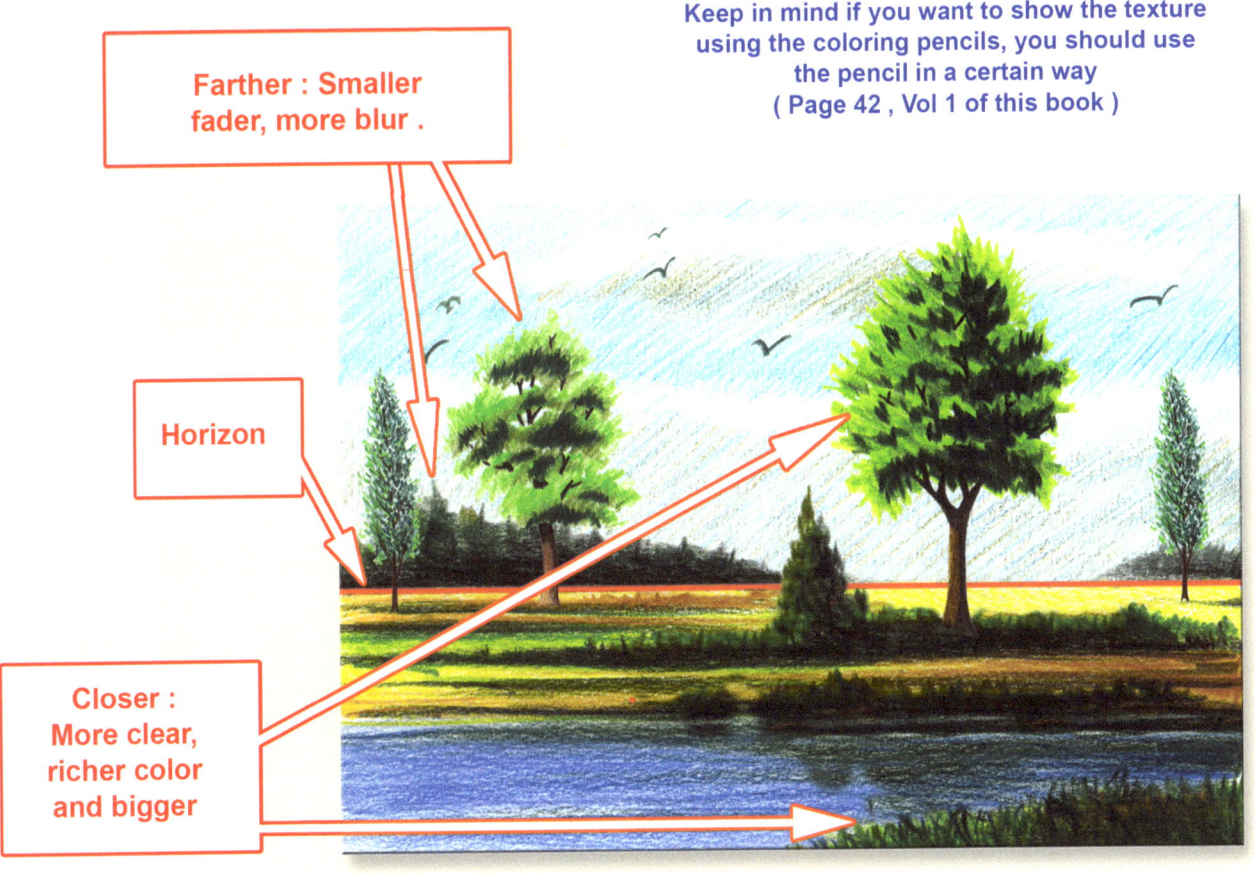

Farther : Smaller fader, more blur .

Horizon

Closer :
More clear, richer color and bigger

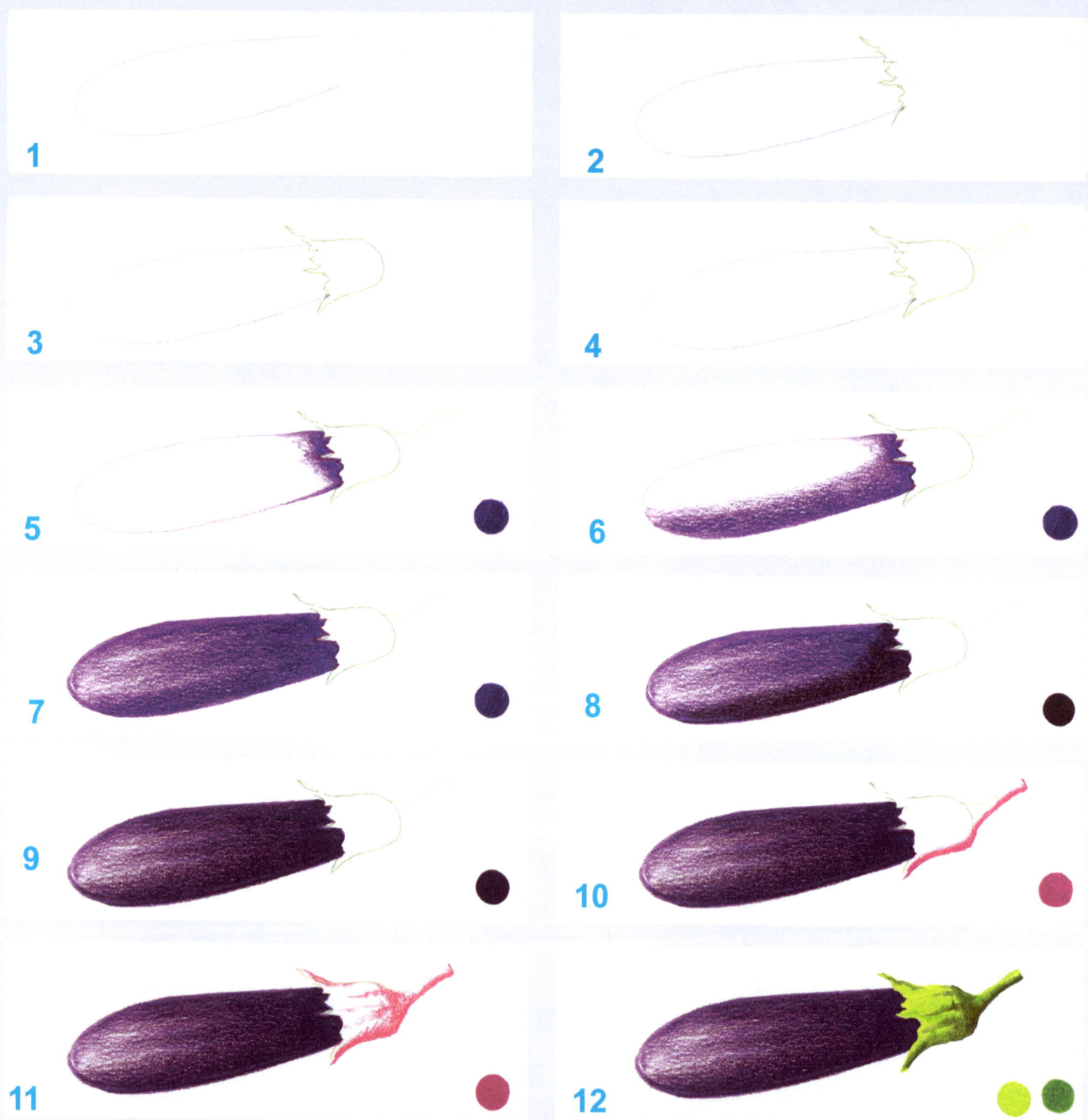

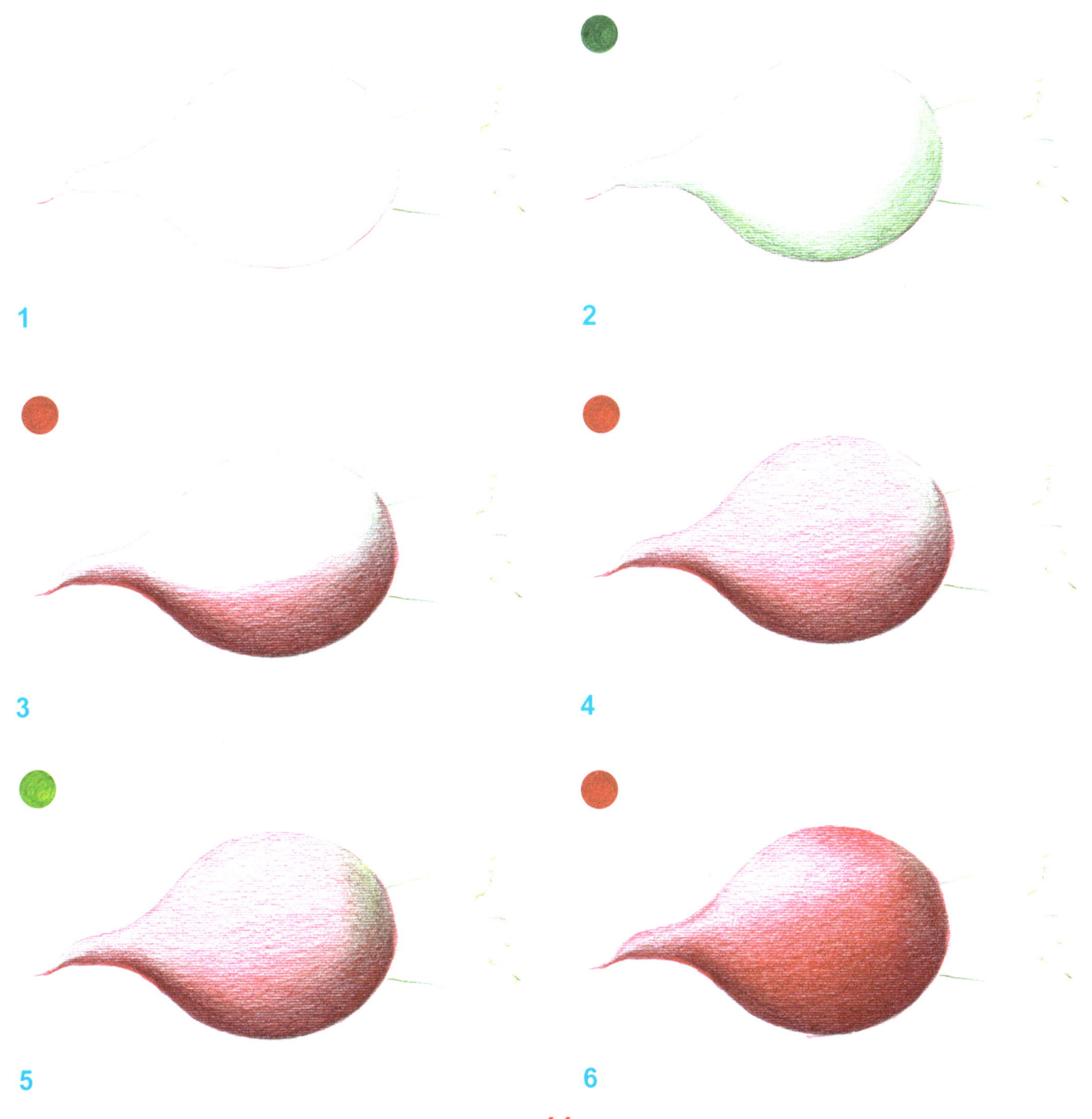

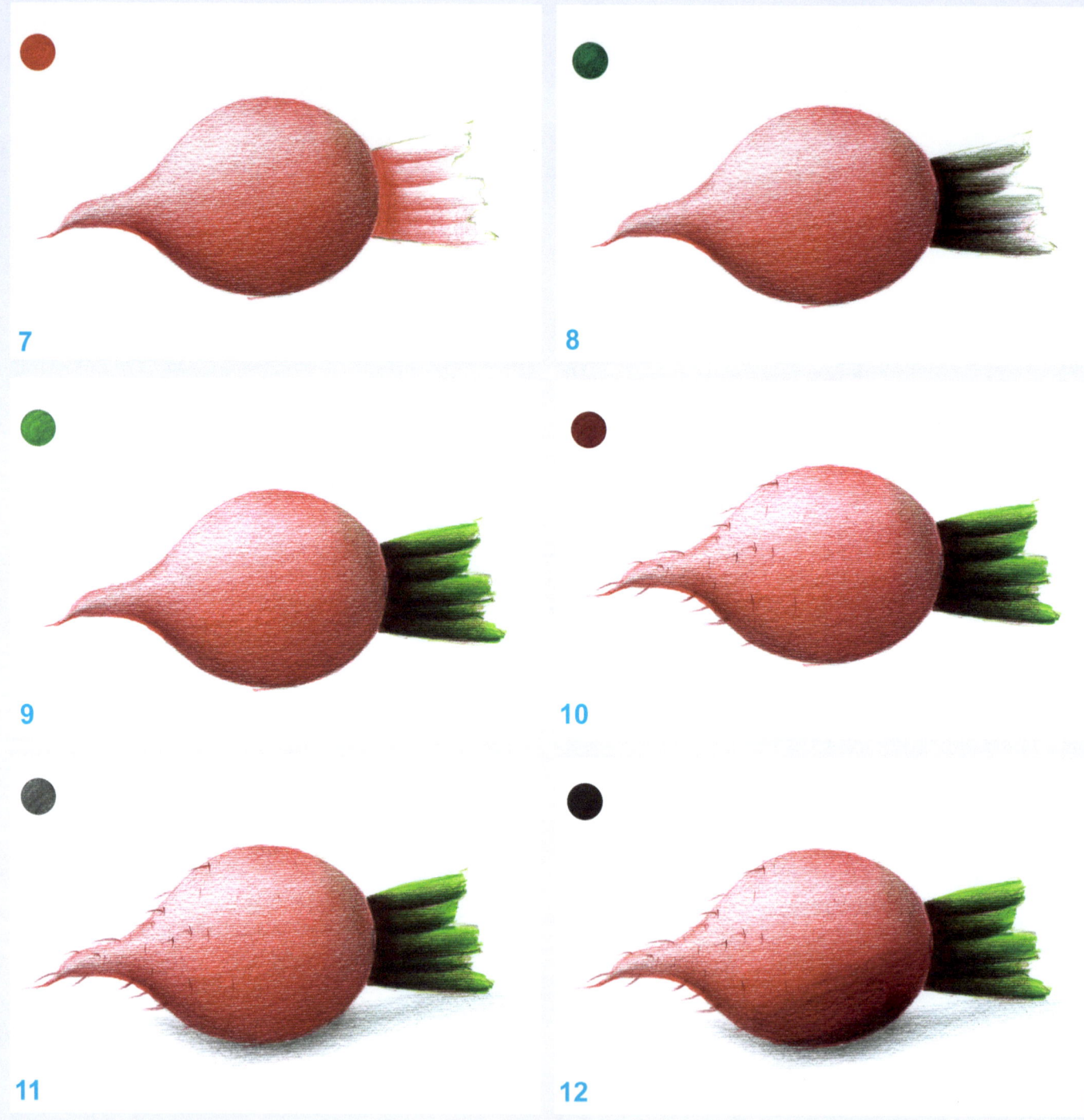

1　　　　　　　　2　　　　　　　　3

4　　　　　　　　5　　　　　　　　6

13

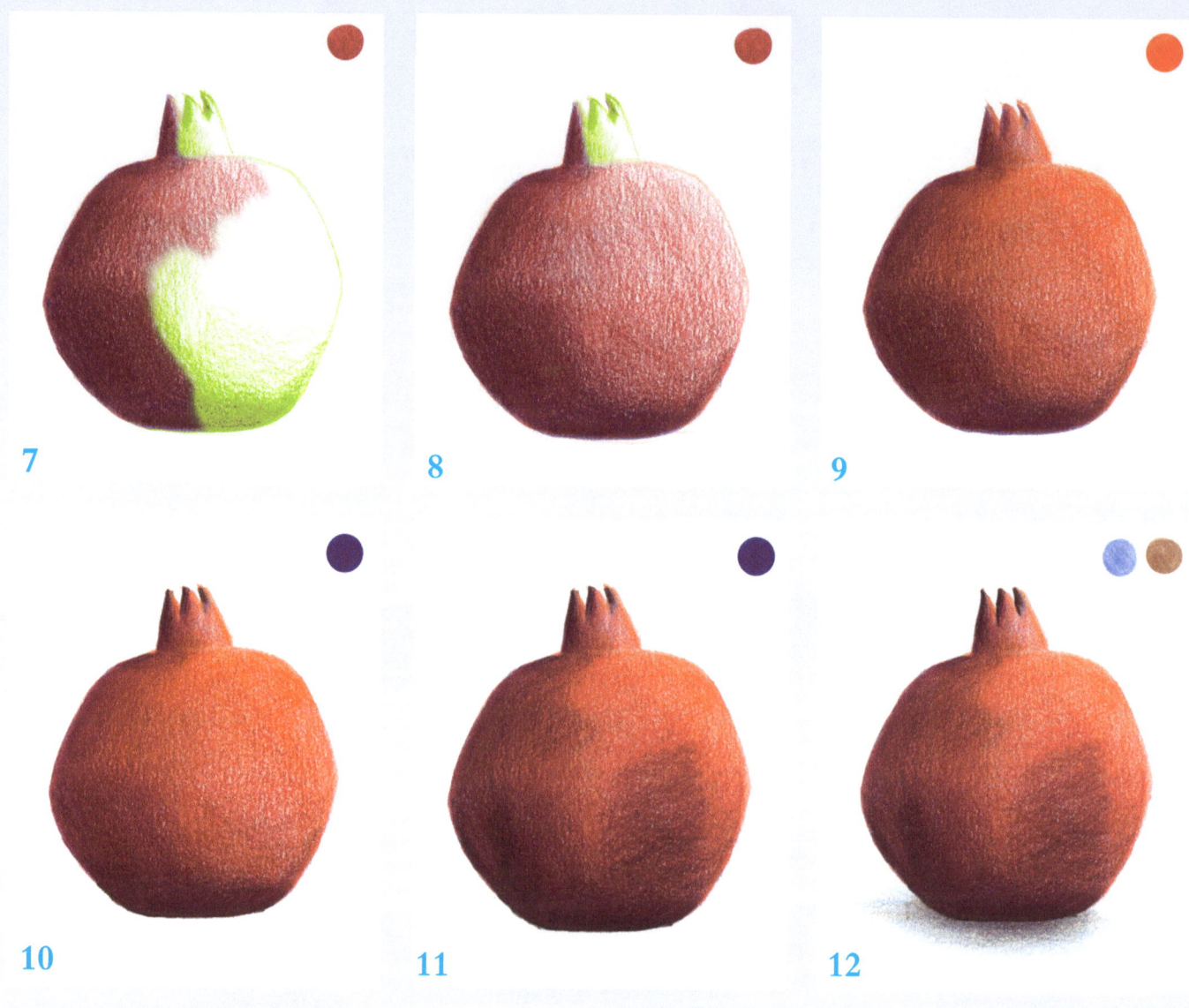

In numbers 10 and 11 use dark colors (Dark purple color) and the tip of pencil and in some parts use the side of the pencil lead to emphasize on the shadow and for number 12 , color the cast shadow (The shadow of the model on ground) using 2 colors

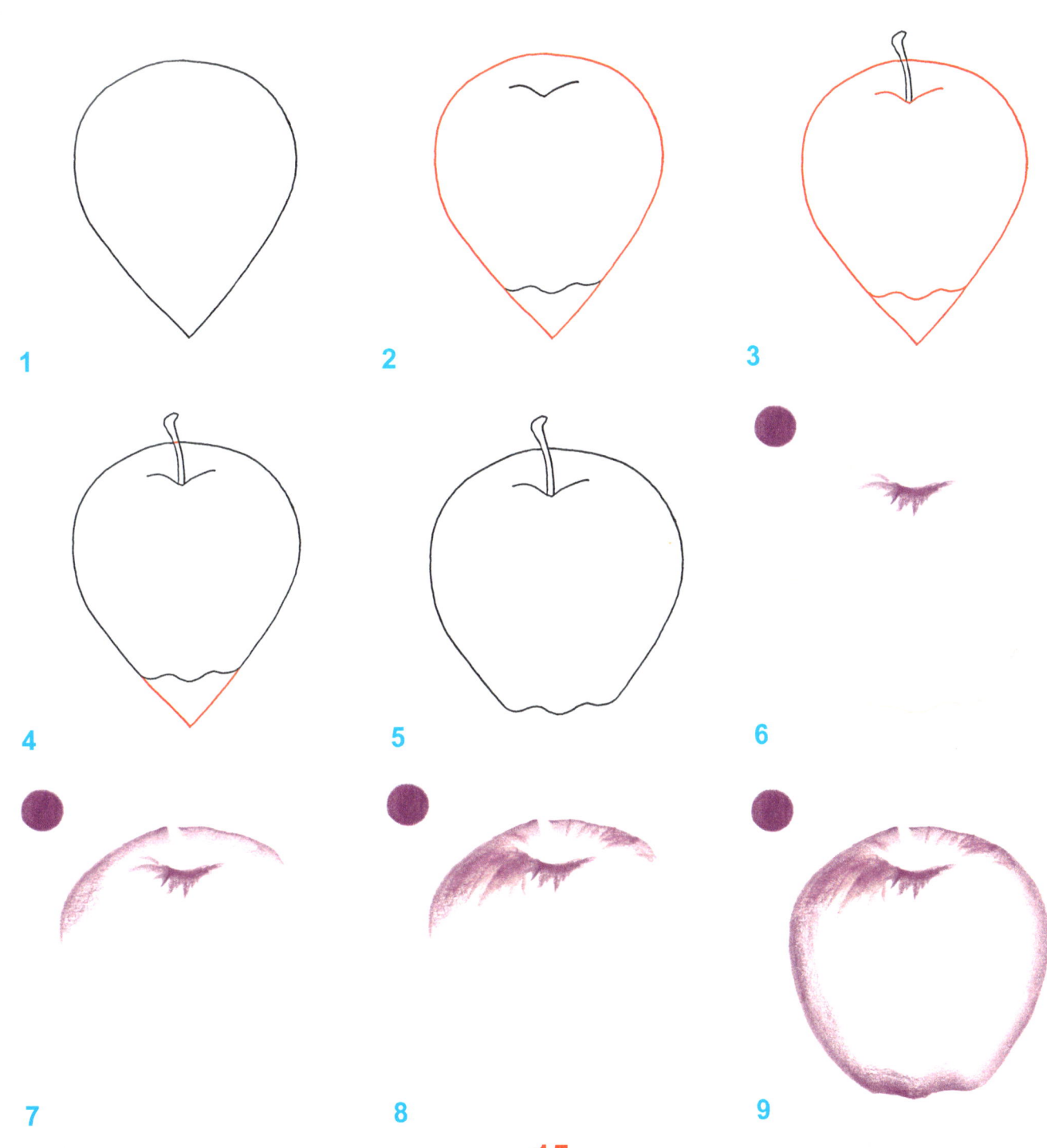

1
2
3
4
5
6
7
8
9

17

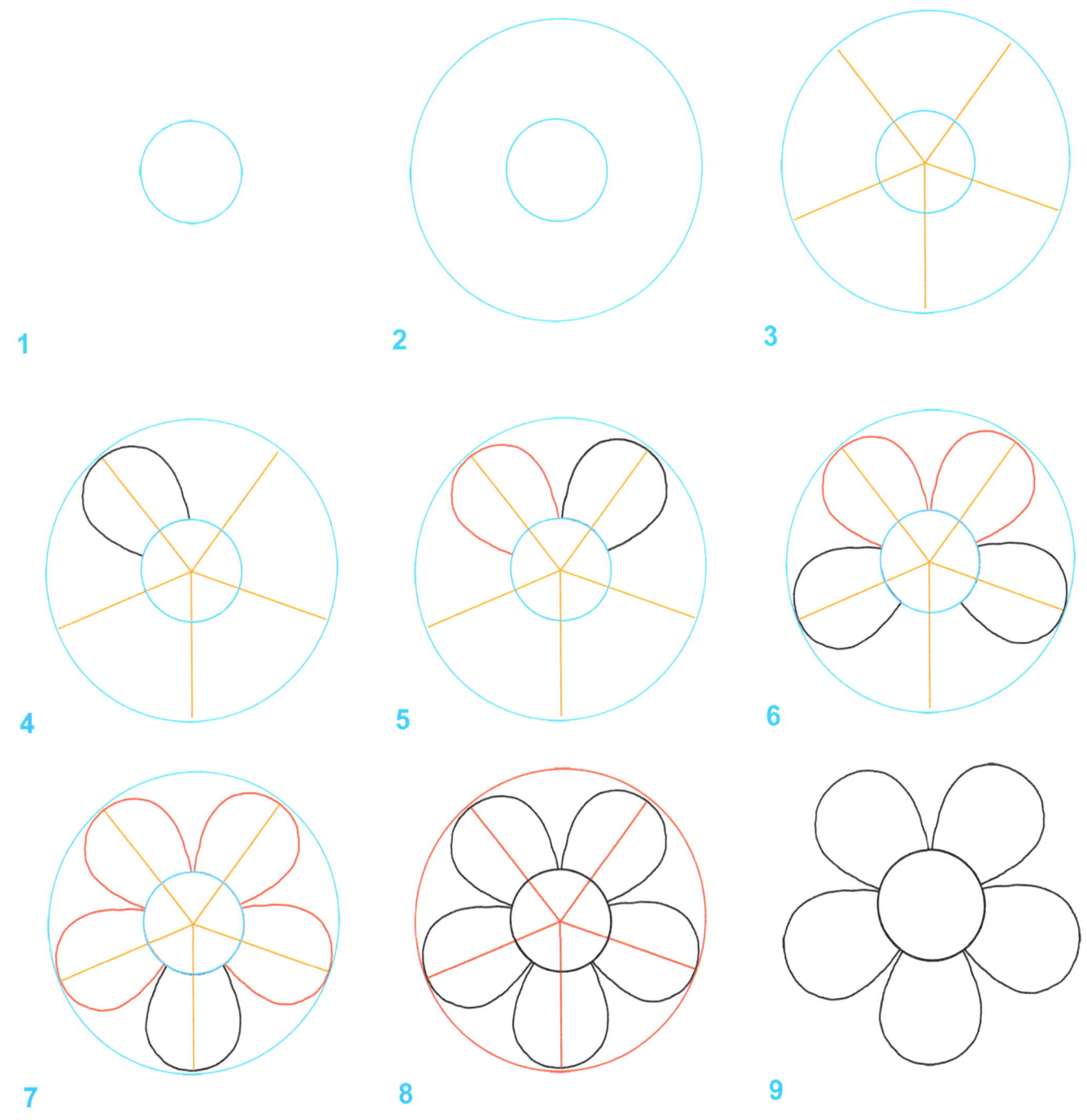

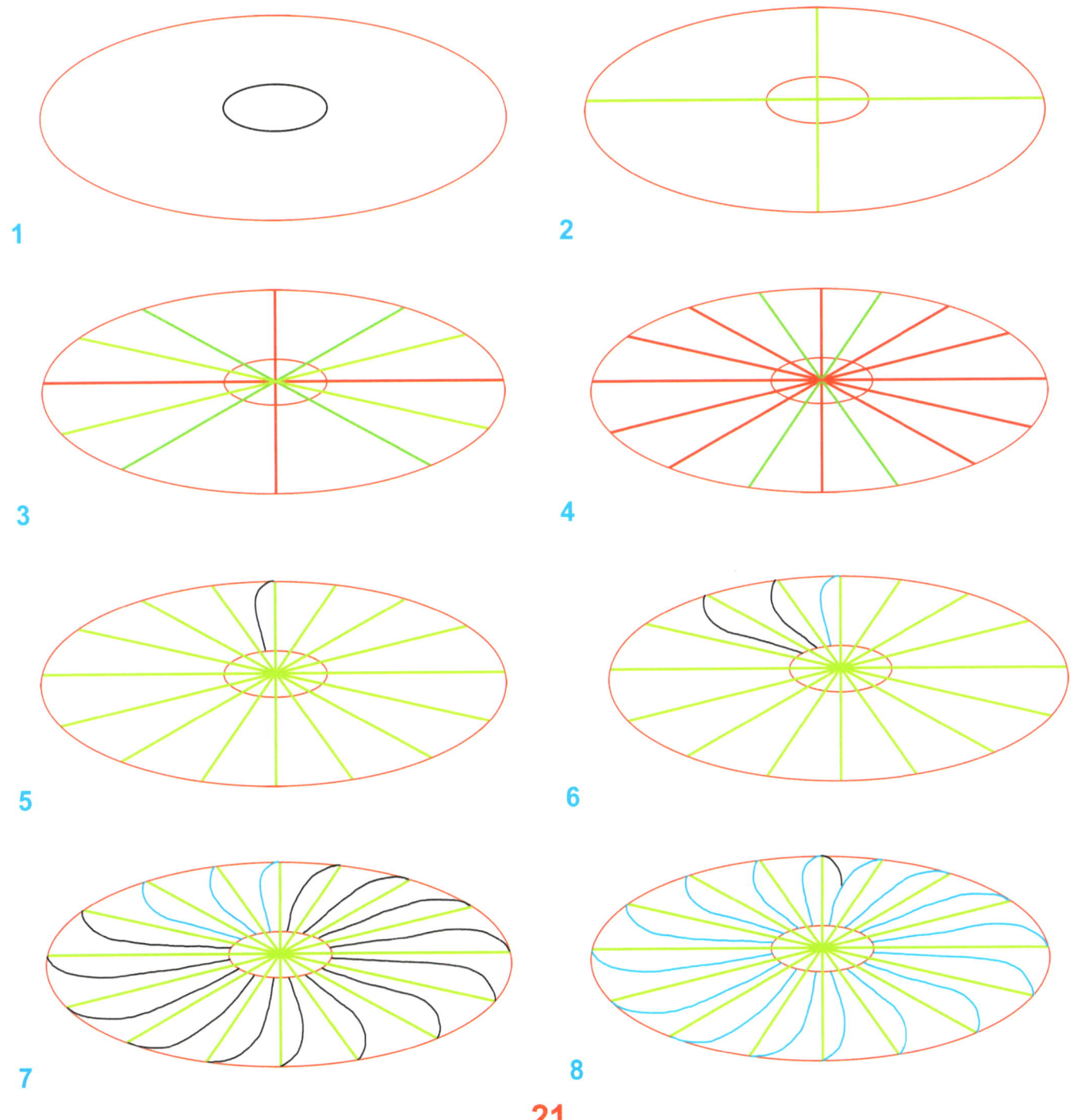

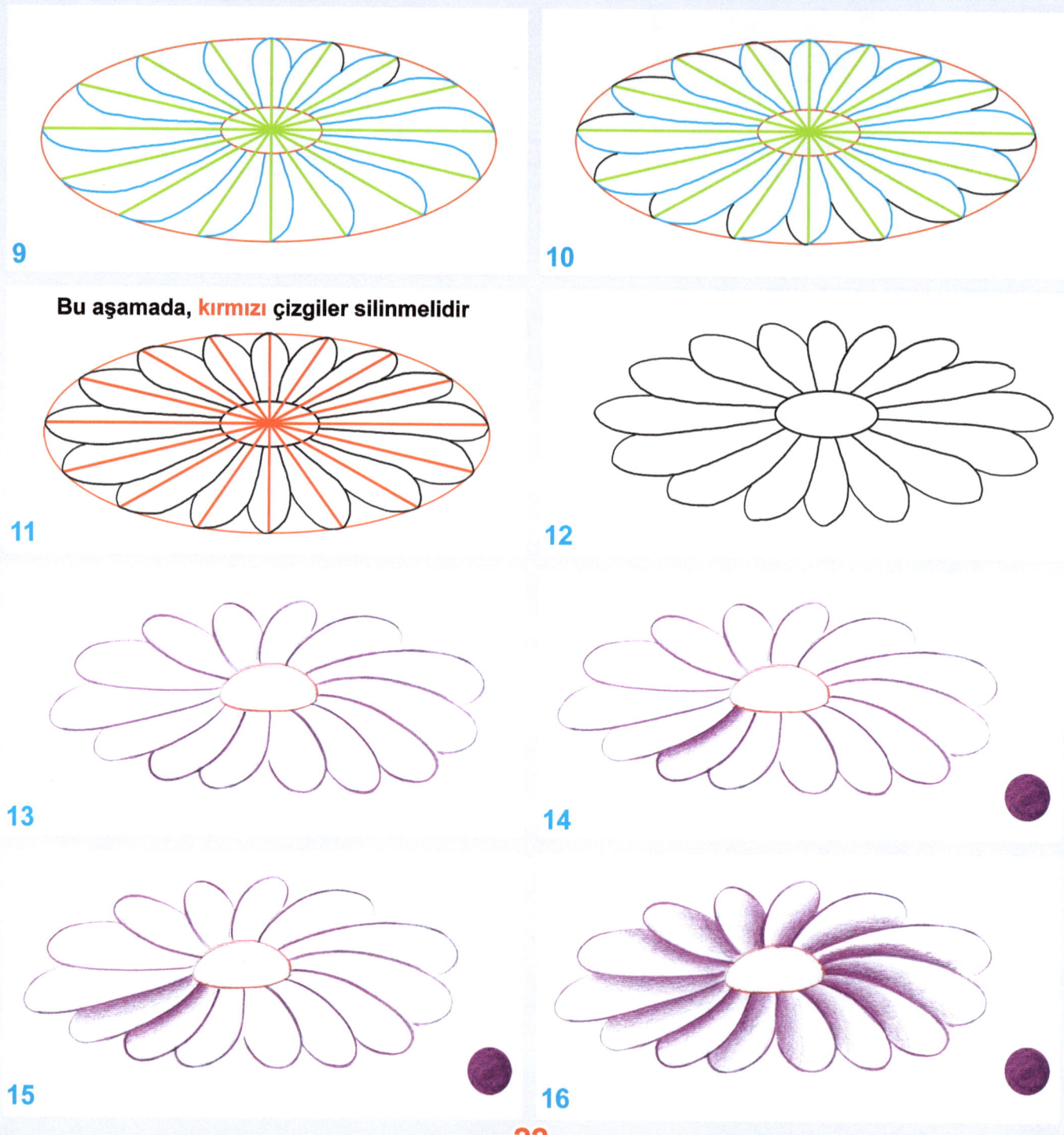

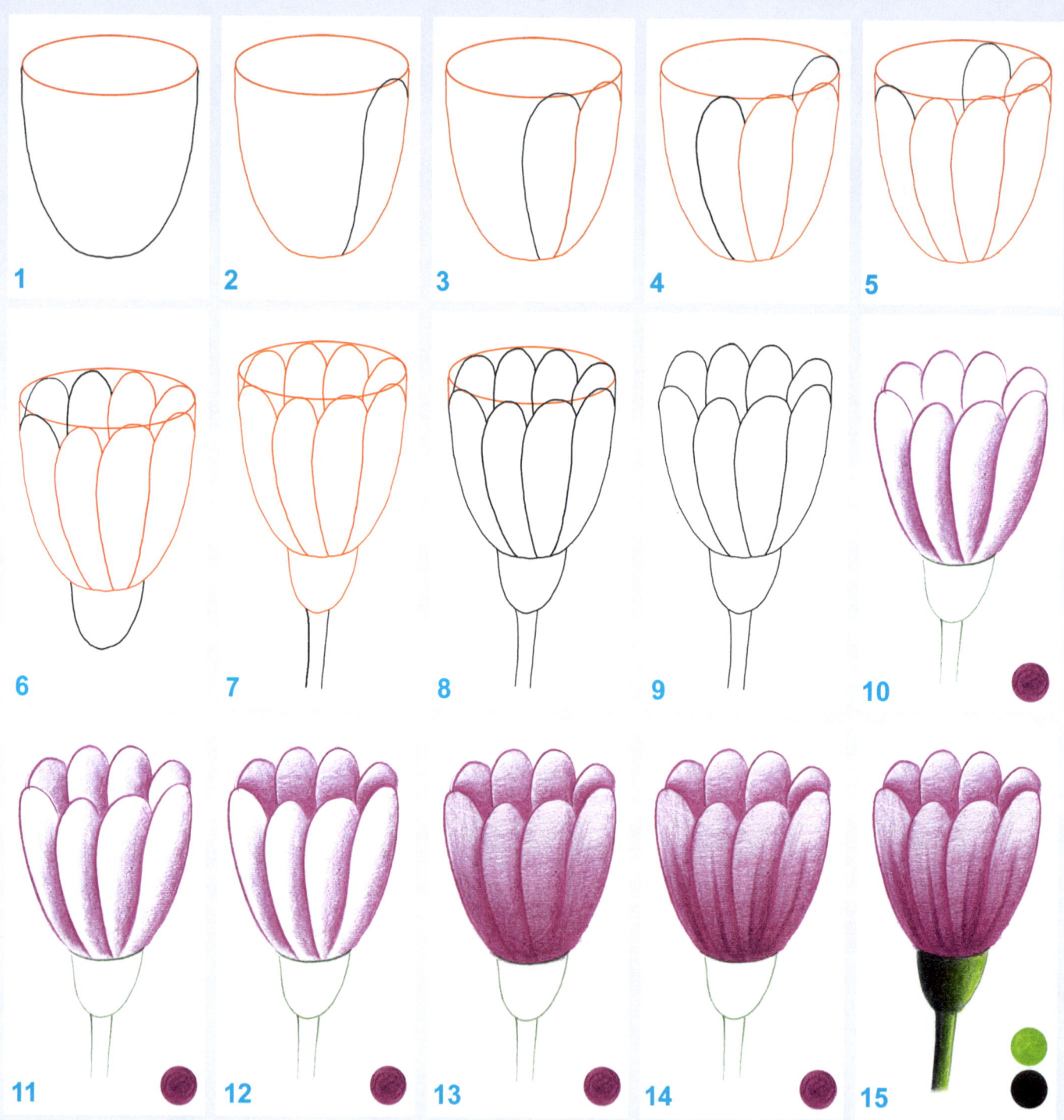

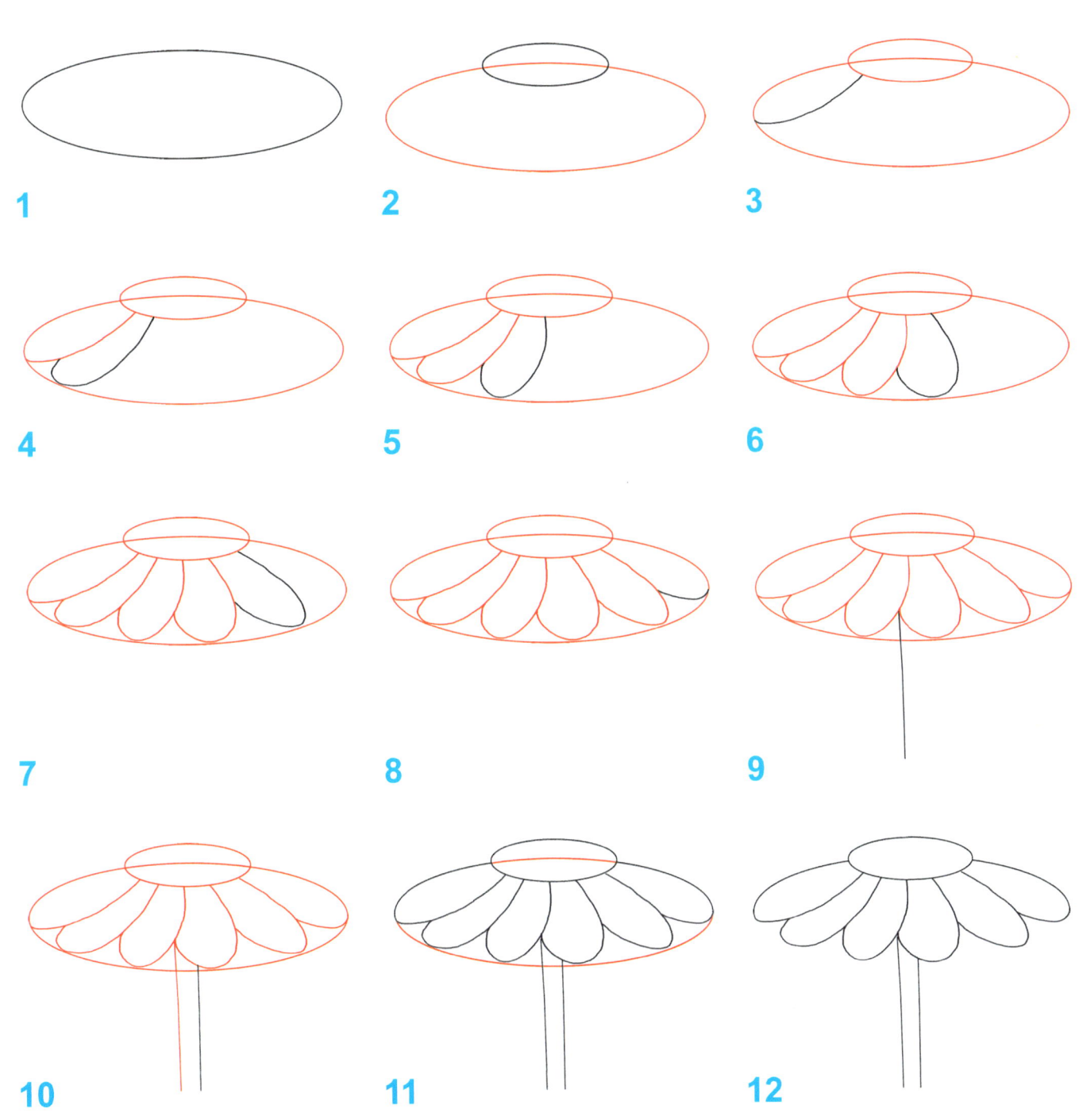

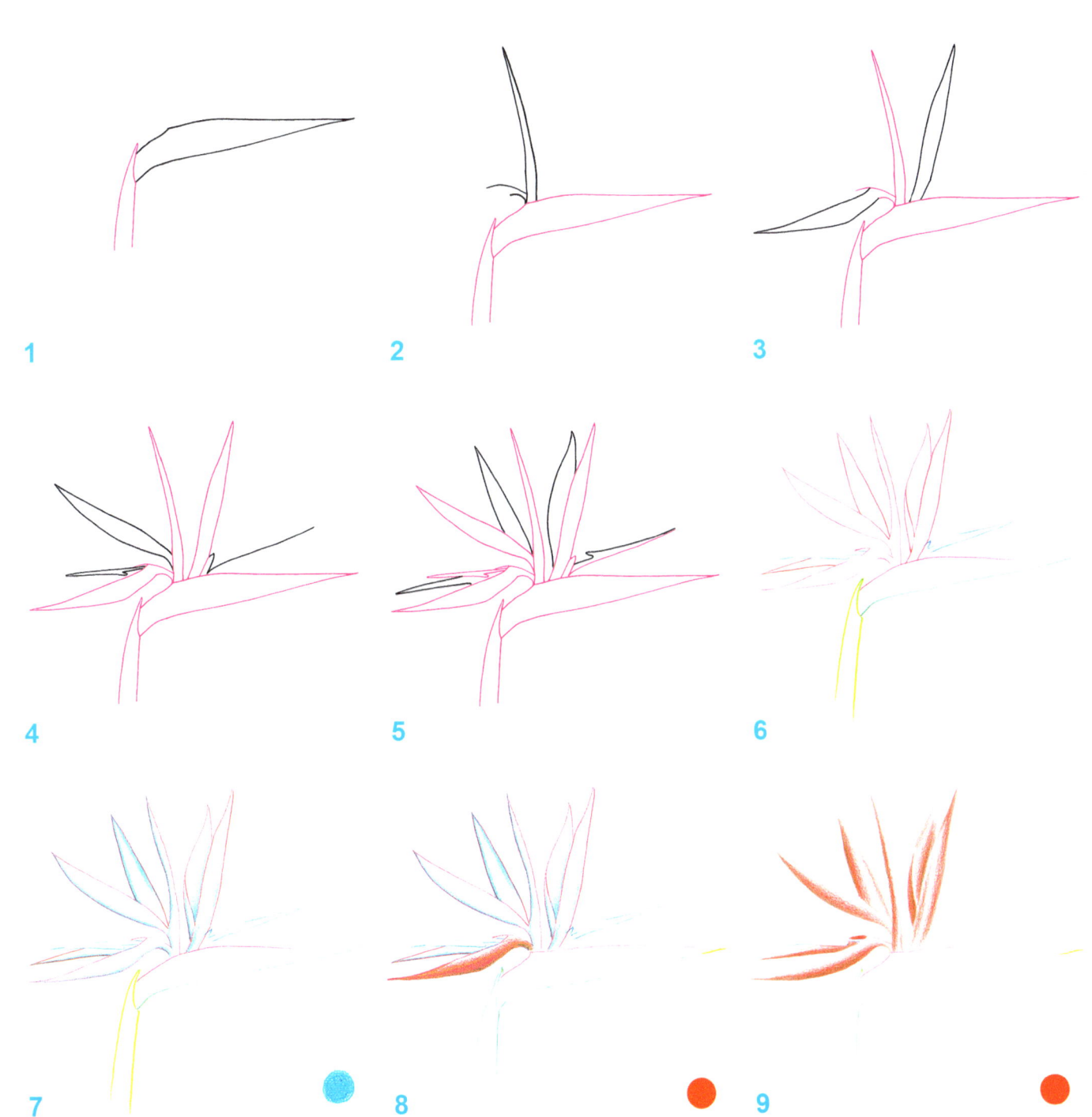

7
8
9
10
11
12

30

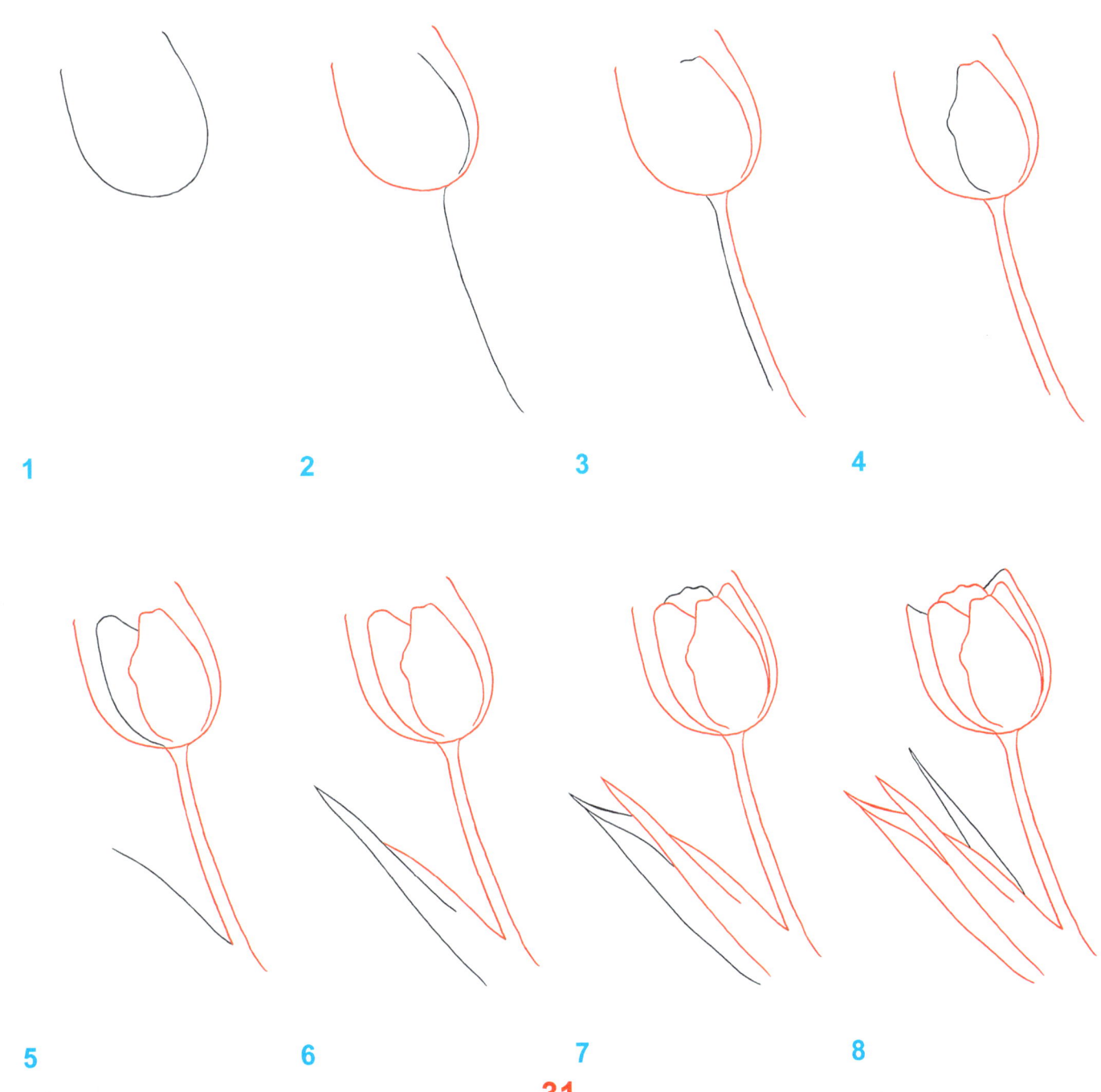

31

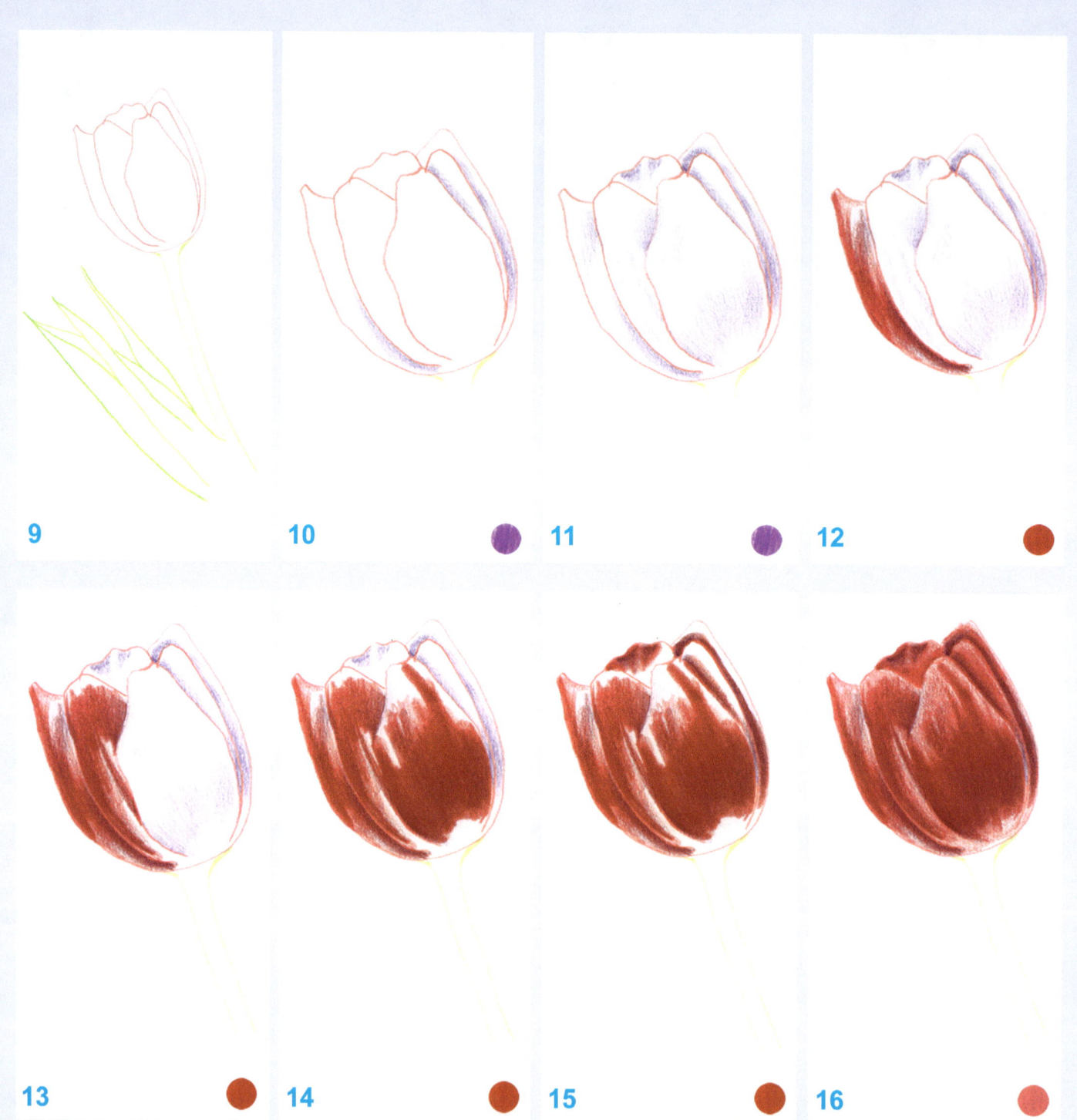

To show an example of using the techniques taught in this book , two painting of objects which we taught separately are kept here as a collection in one piece .

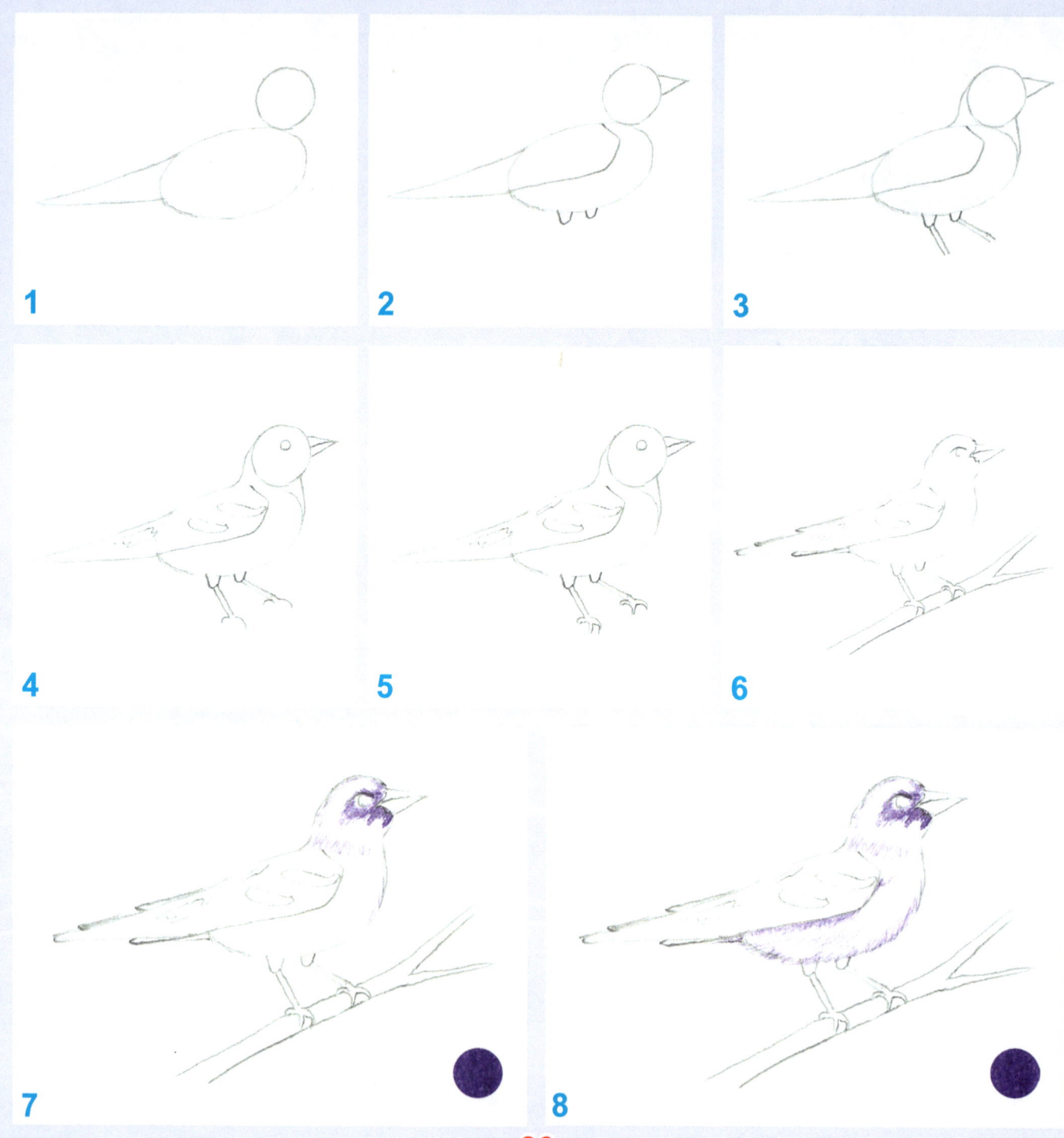

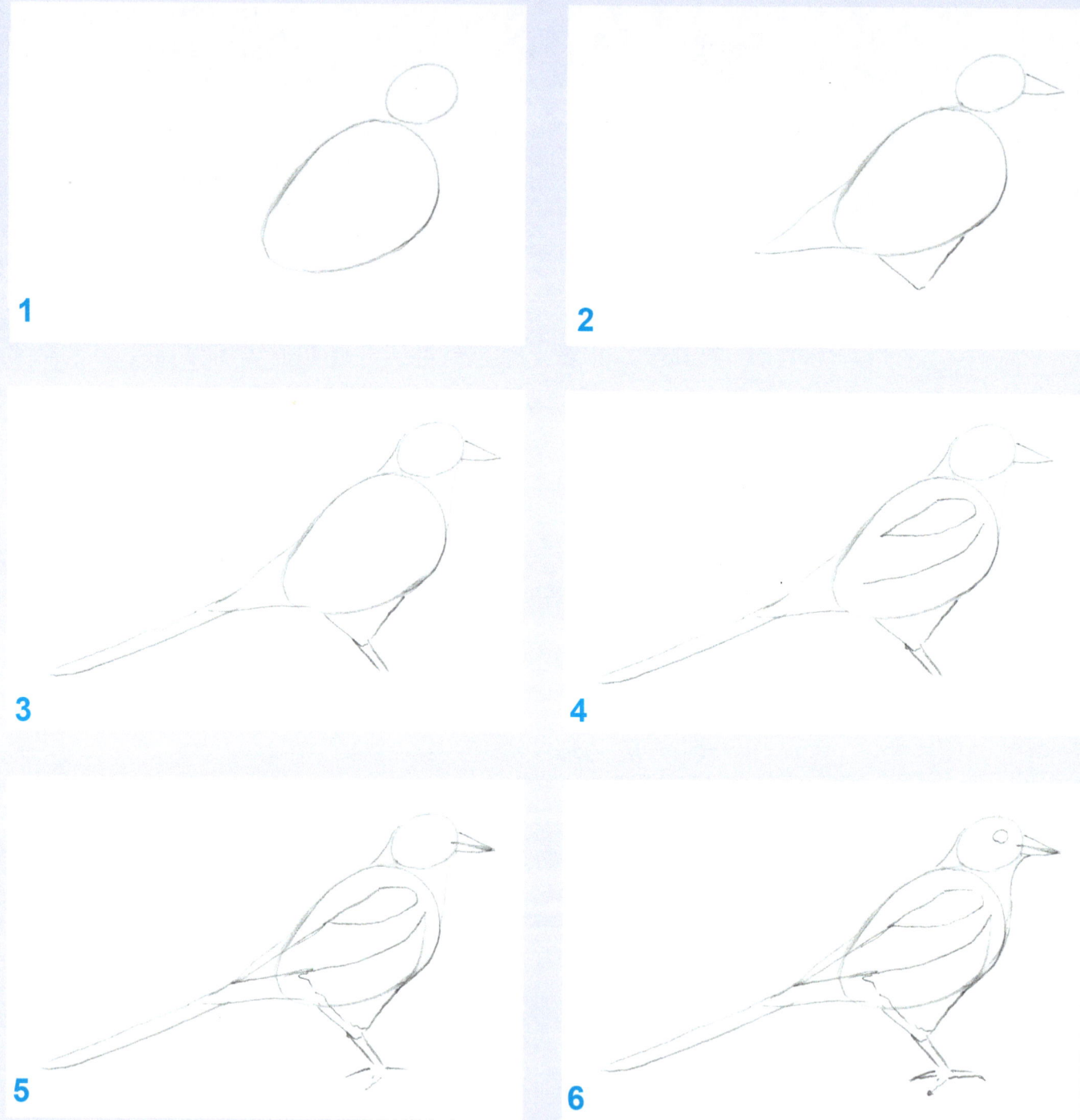

By using what you have learned in the previous lessons ,

you can create a beautiful painting ,

so you and your loved ones can enjoy your art .

7 8 9

10 11 12

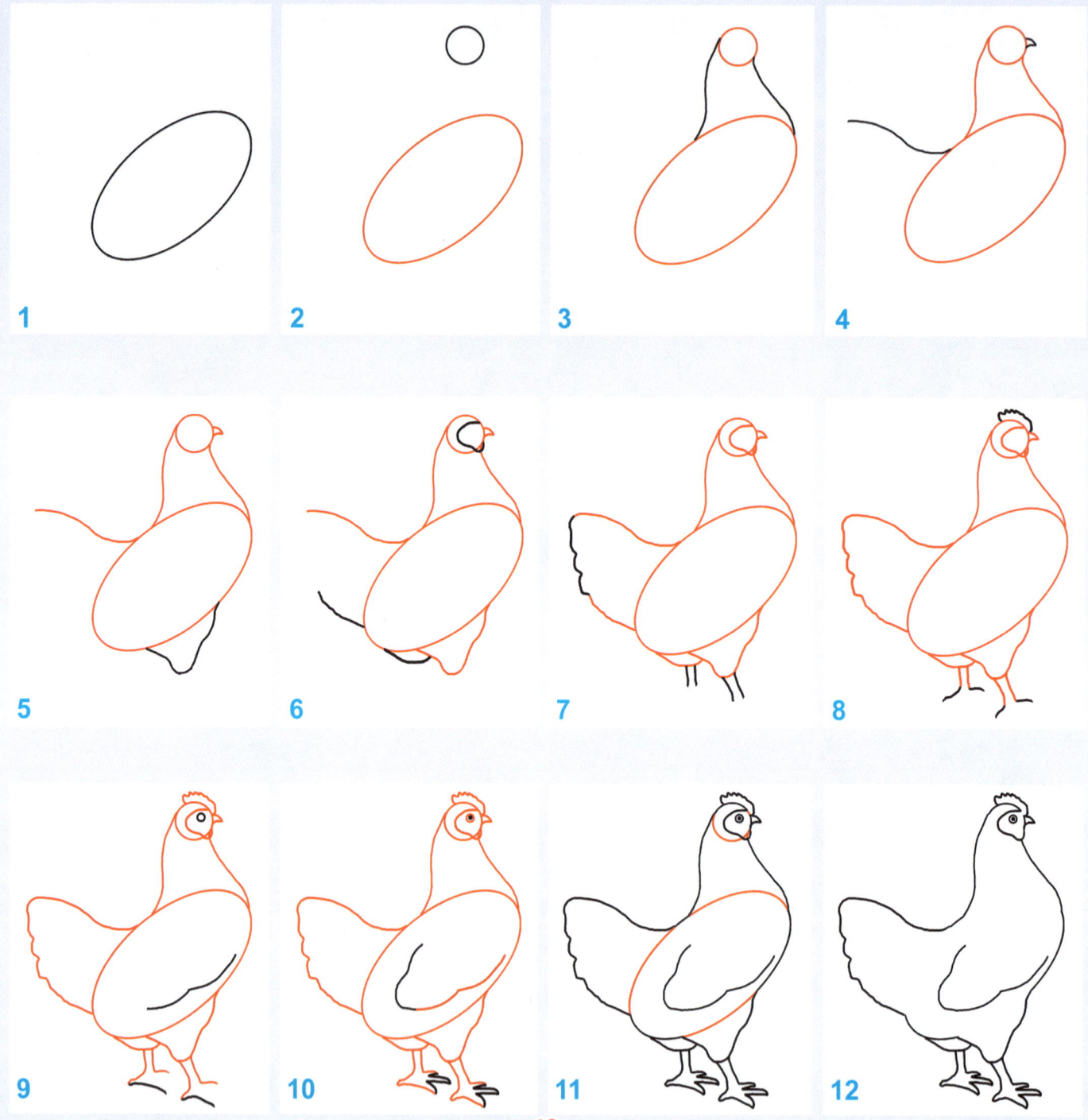

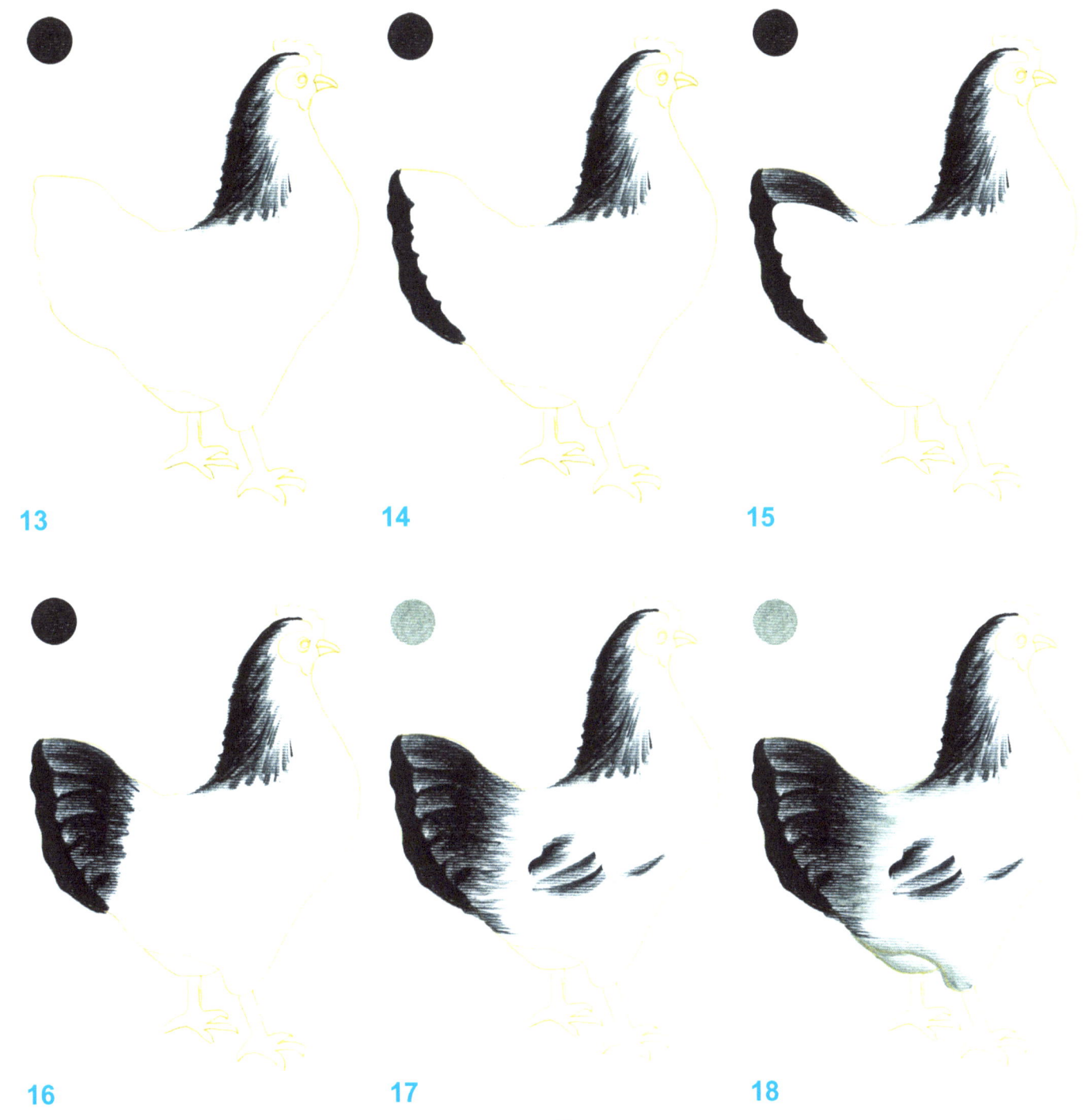

19   20   21

21   22   23

50

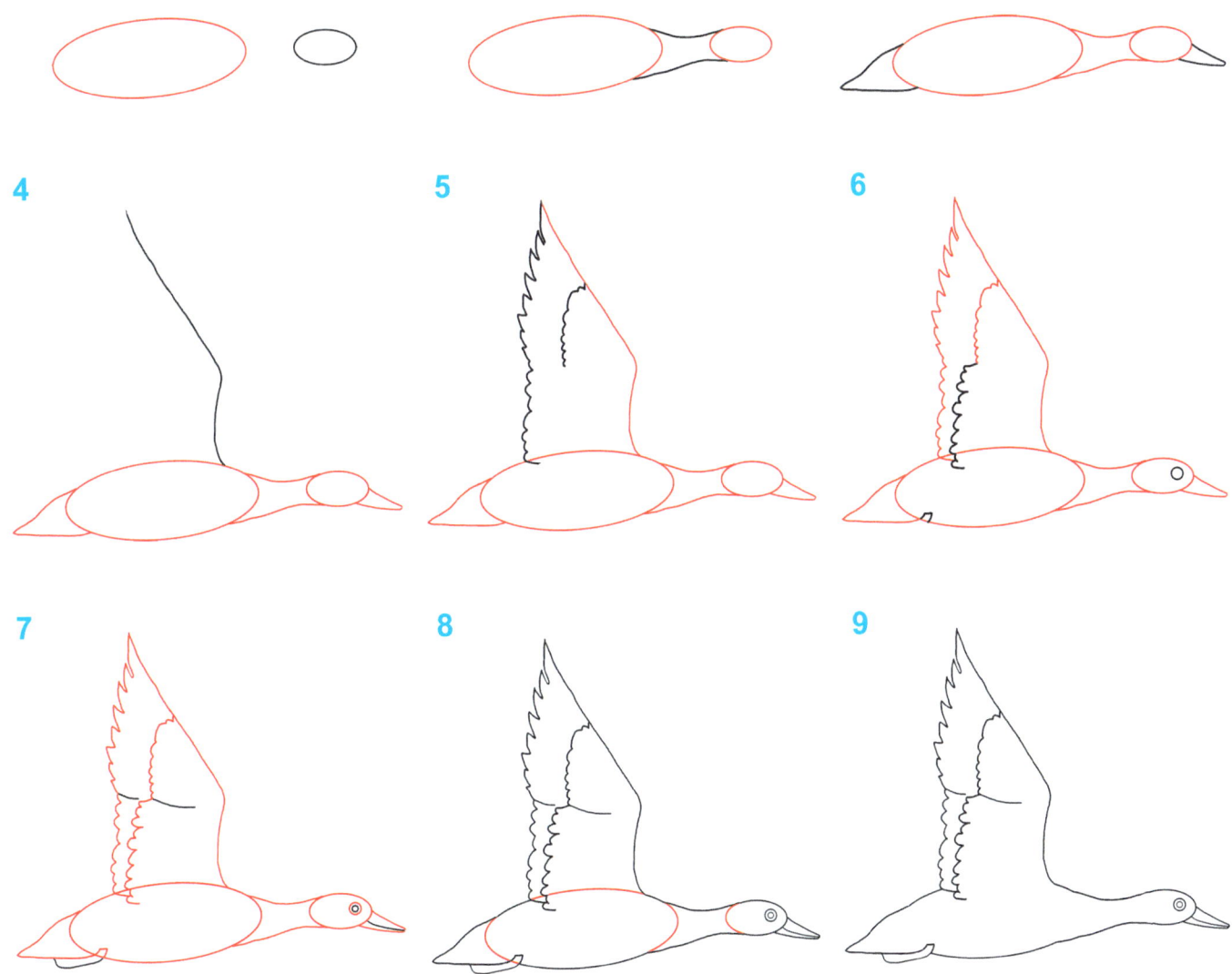

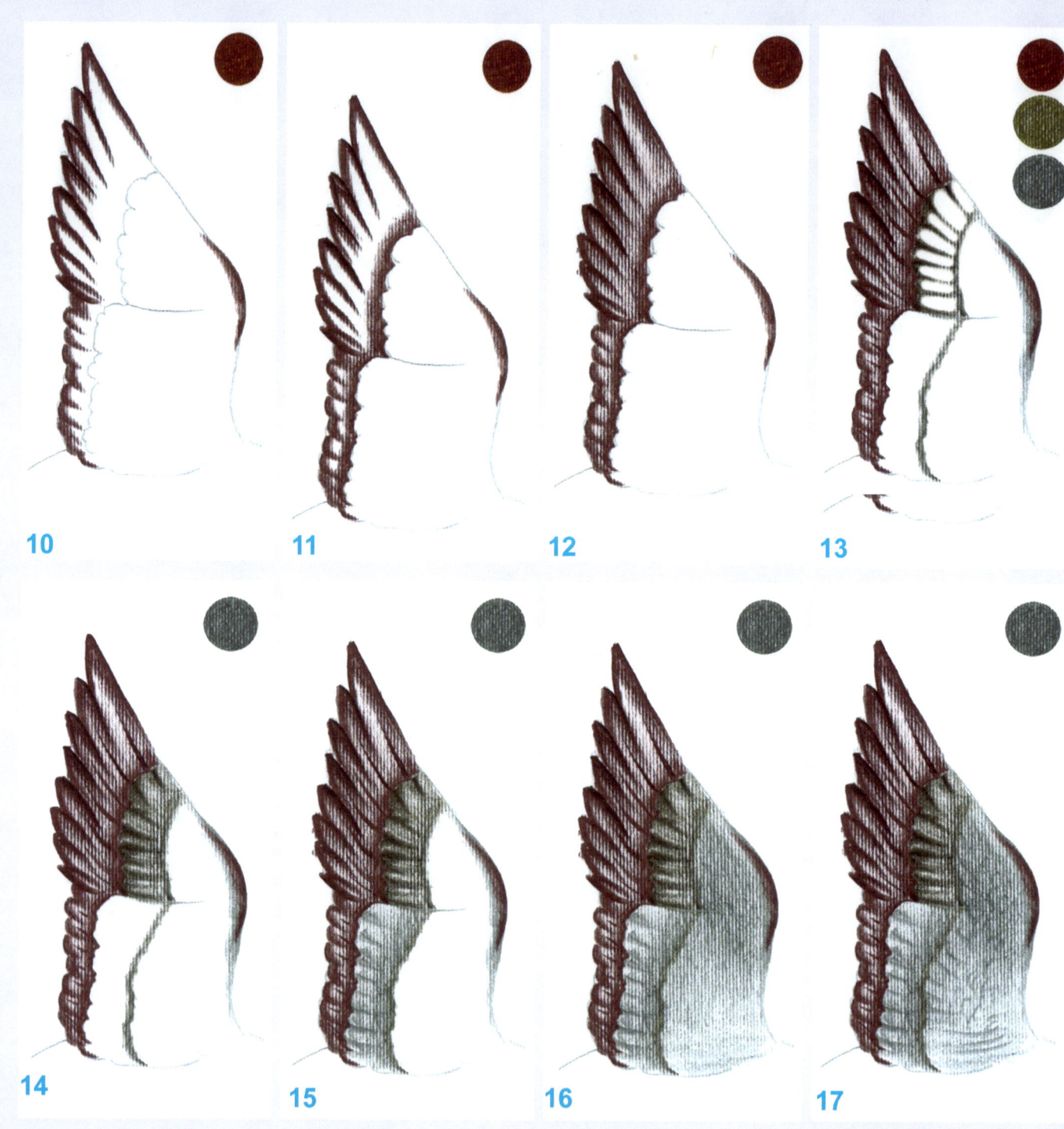

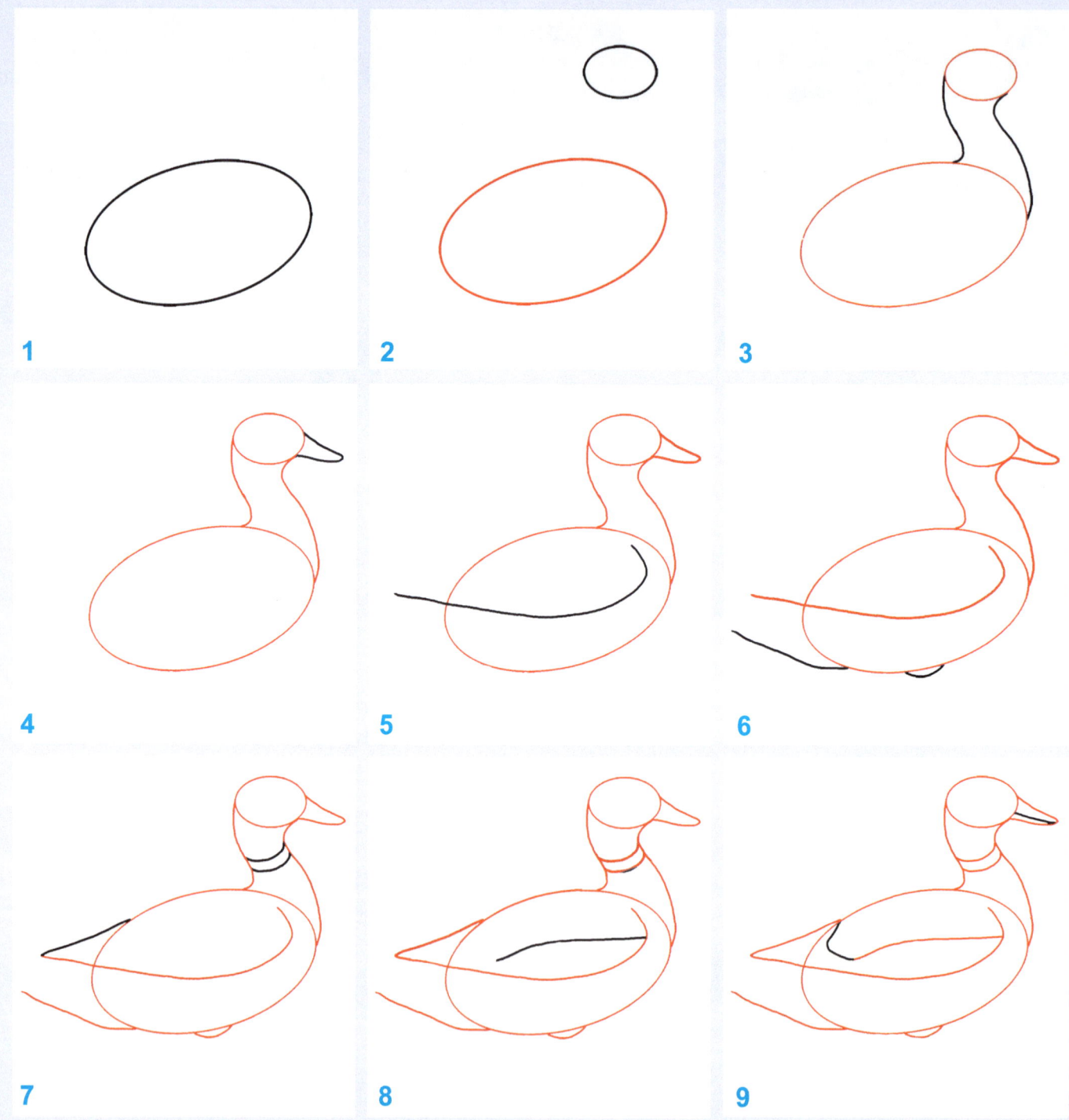

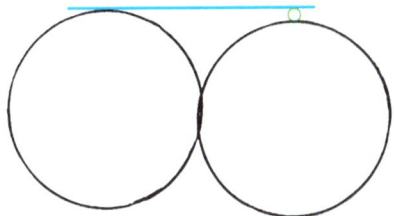

1

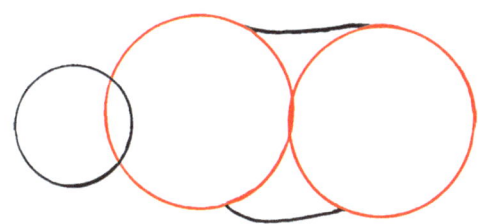

2

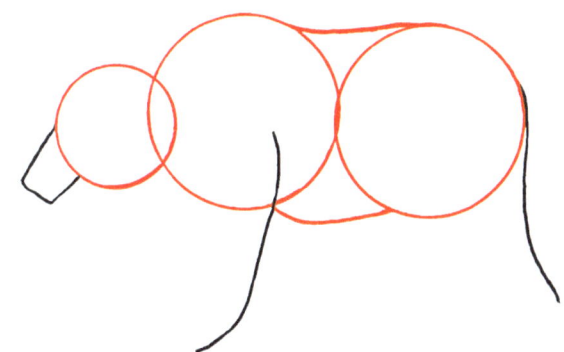

3

4

5

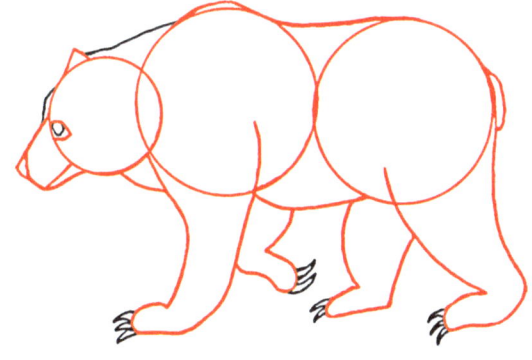

6

7

8

9

10

11

12

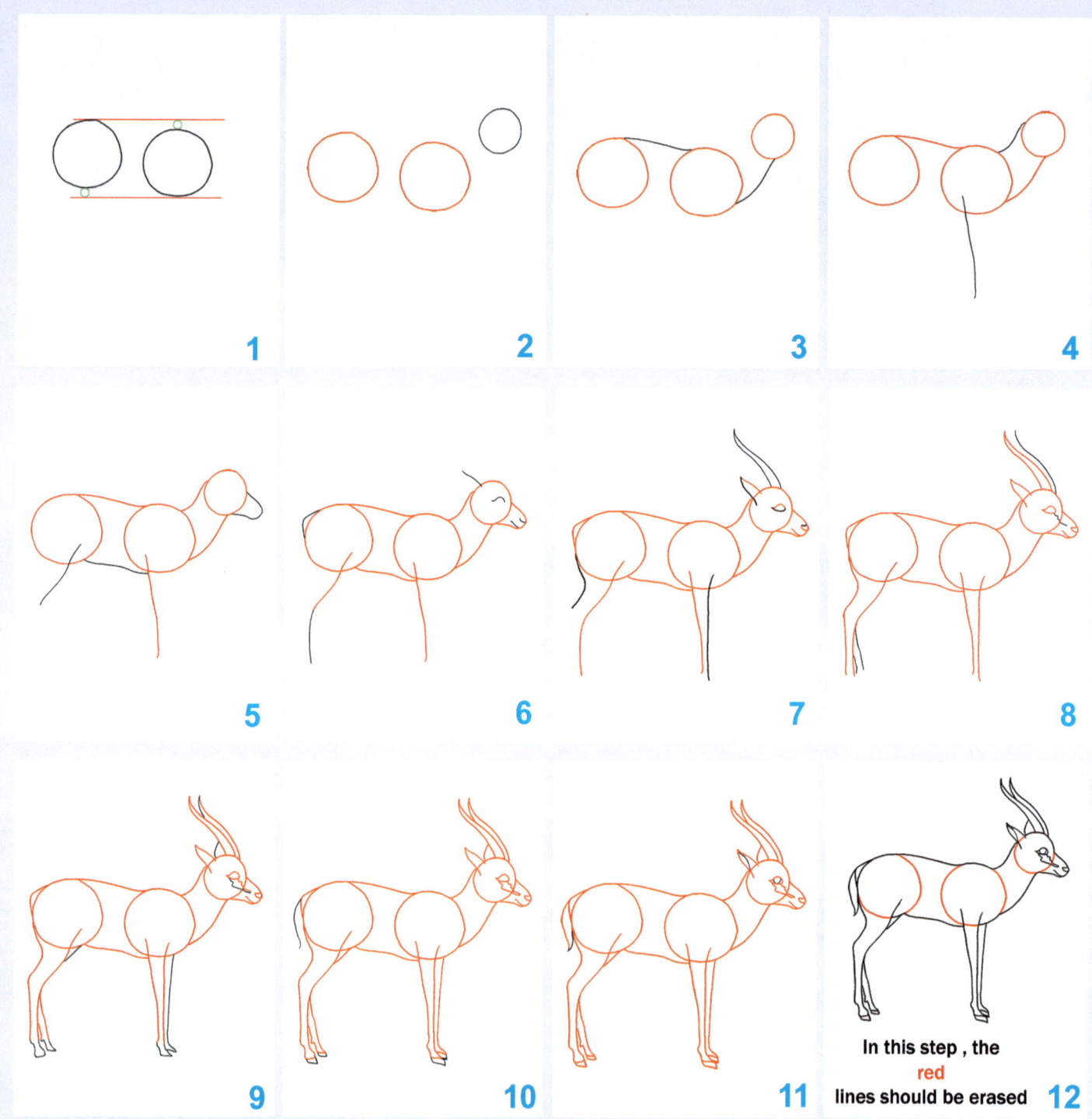

17

18

19

20

21

22

23

24

1

2

3

4

5

64

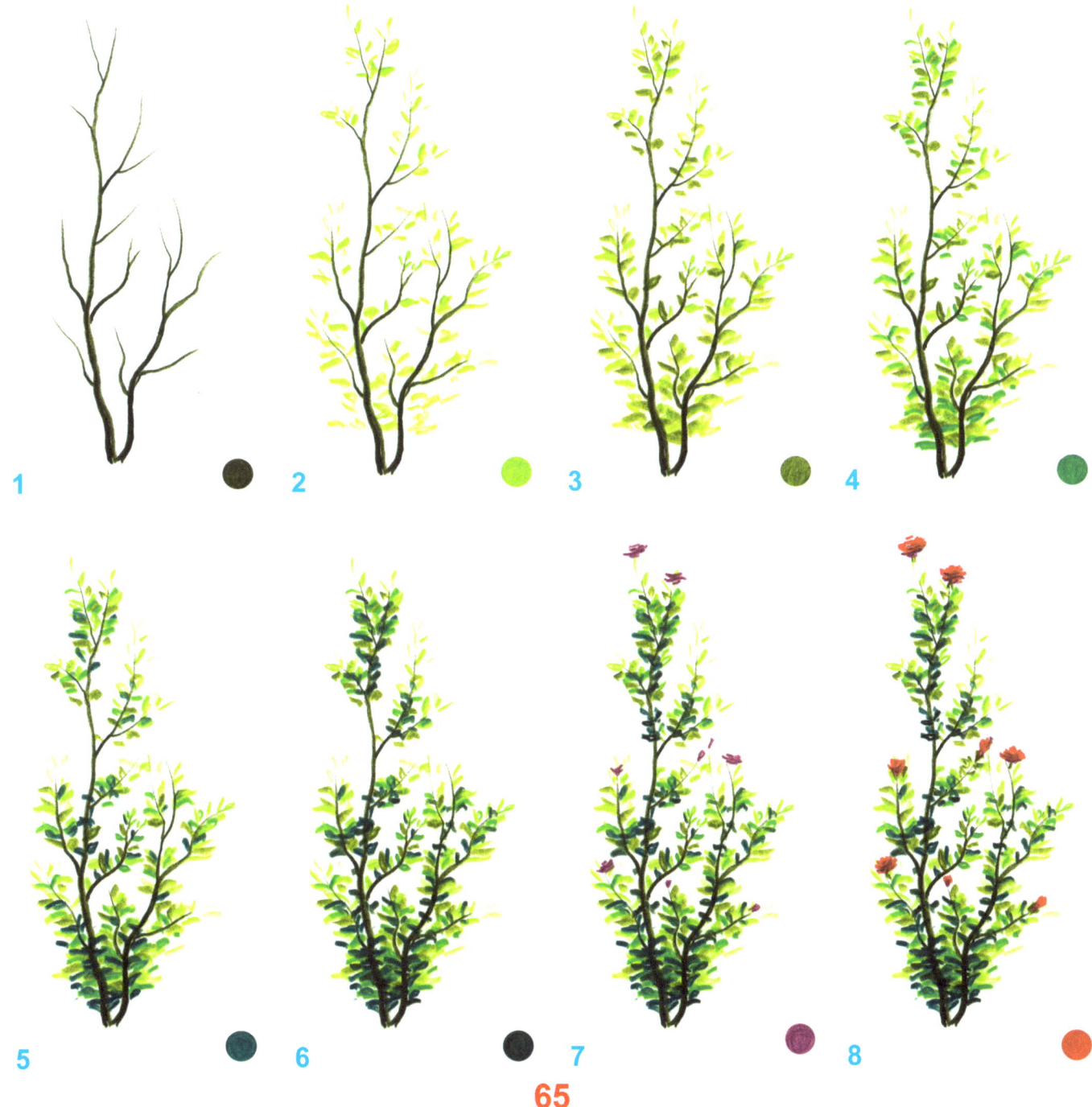

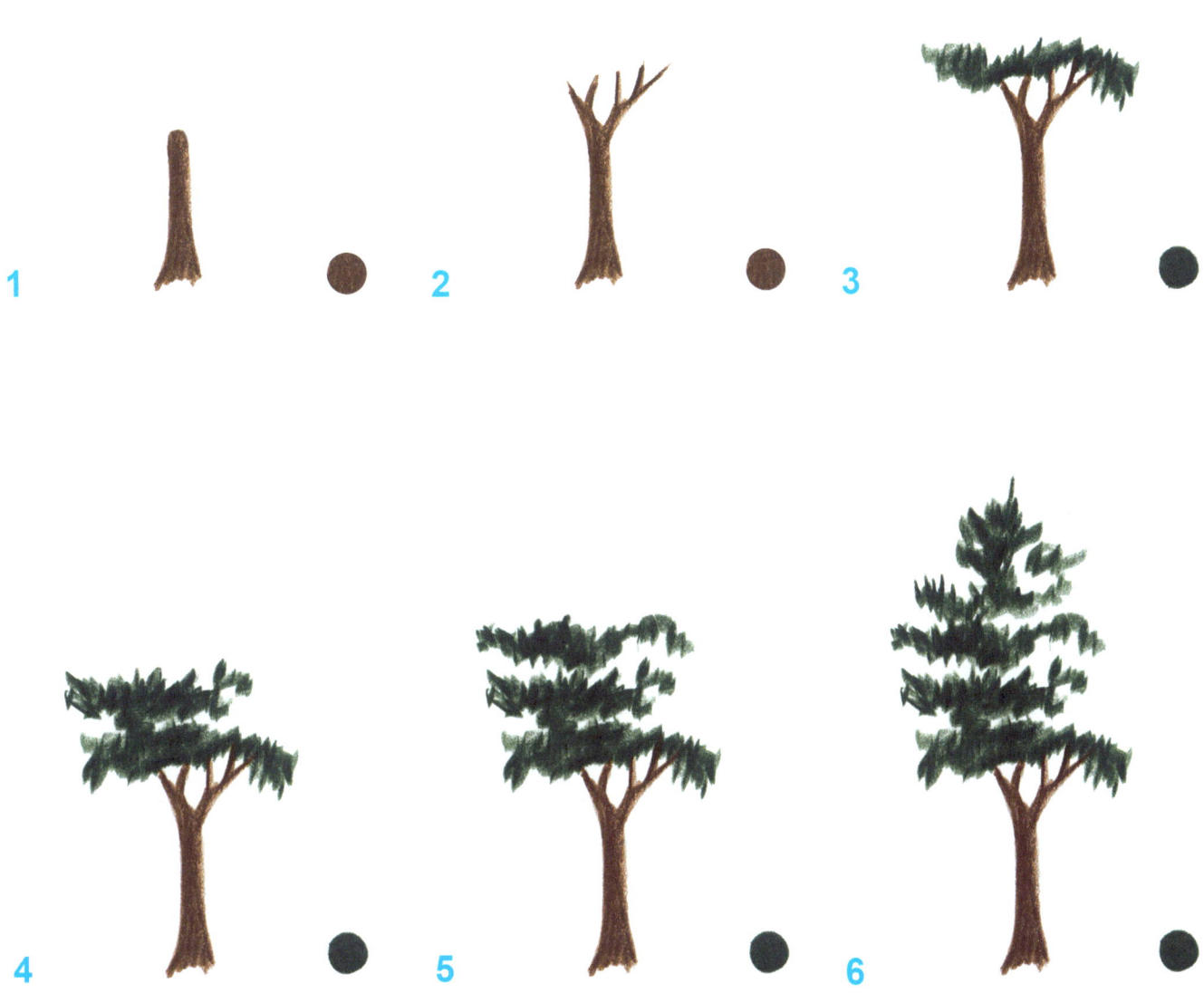

7    8    9

10    11    12

68

69

71

10

11

12

1

2

3

4

5

6

73

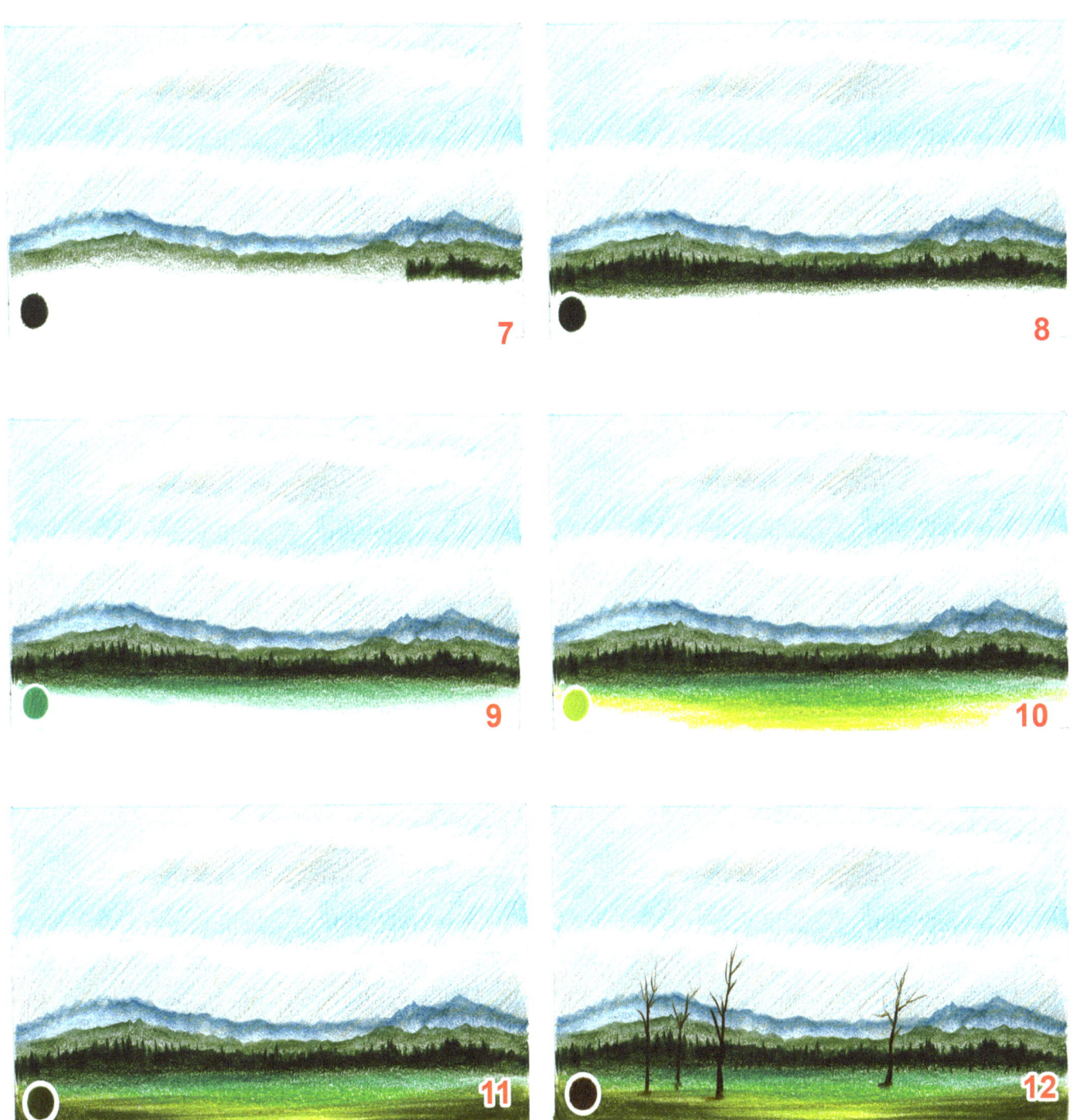

13

14

8

9

10

11

78

12

13

14

79

13

14

Creating landscape is one of the common topics of Drawing and Painting .
Learning to study and paint its details such as tree, bush, grass… is very necessary .

7

8

9

10

11

12

84

To draw nature in different seasons you should use the colors of that particular season such as the two above paintings in which warm colors have been used

By combining the details of nature nd the colors of that season you can create beautiful scenery . We have presented samples of them .

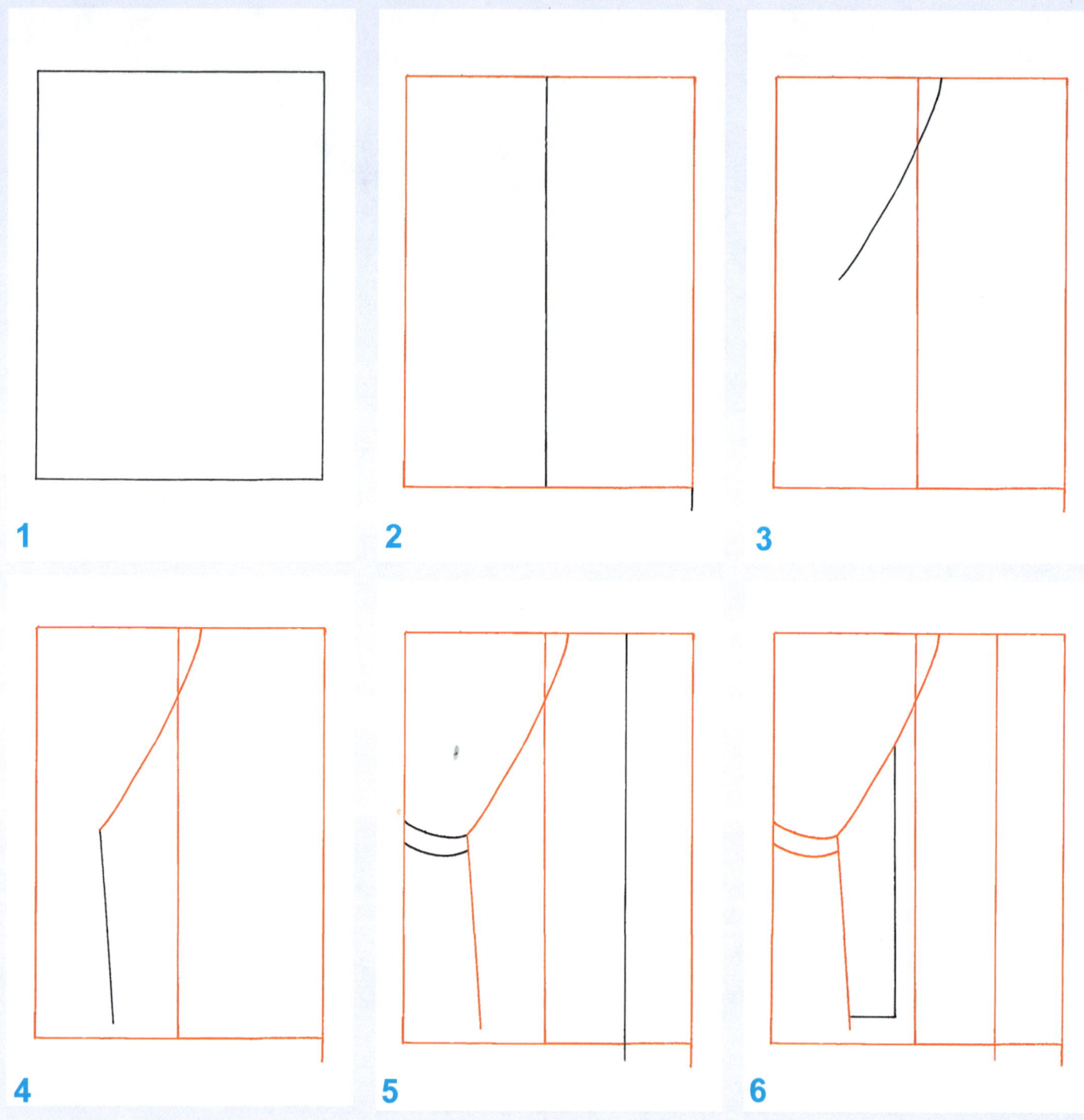

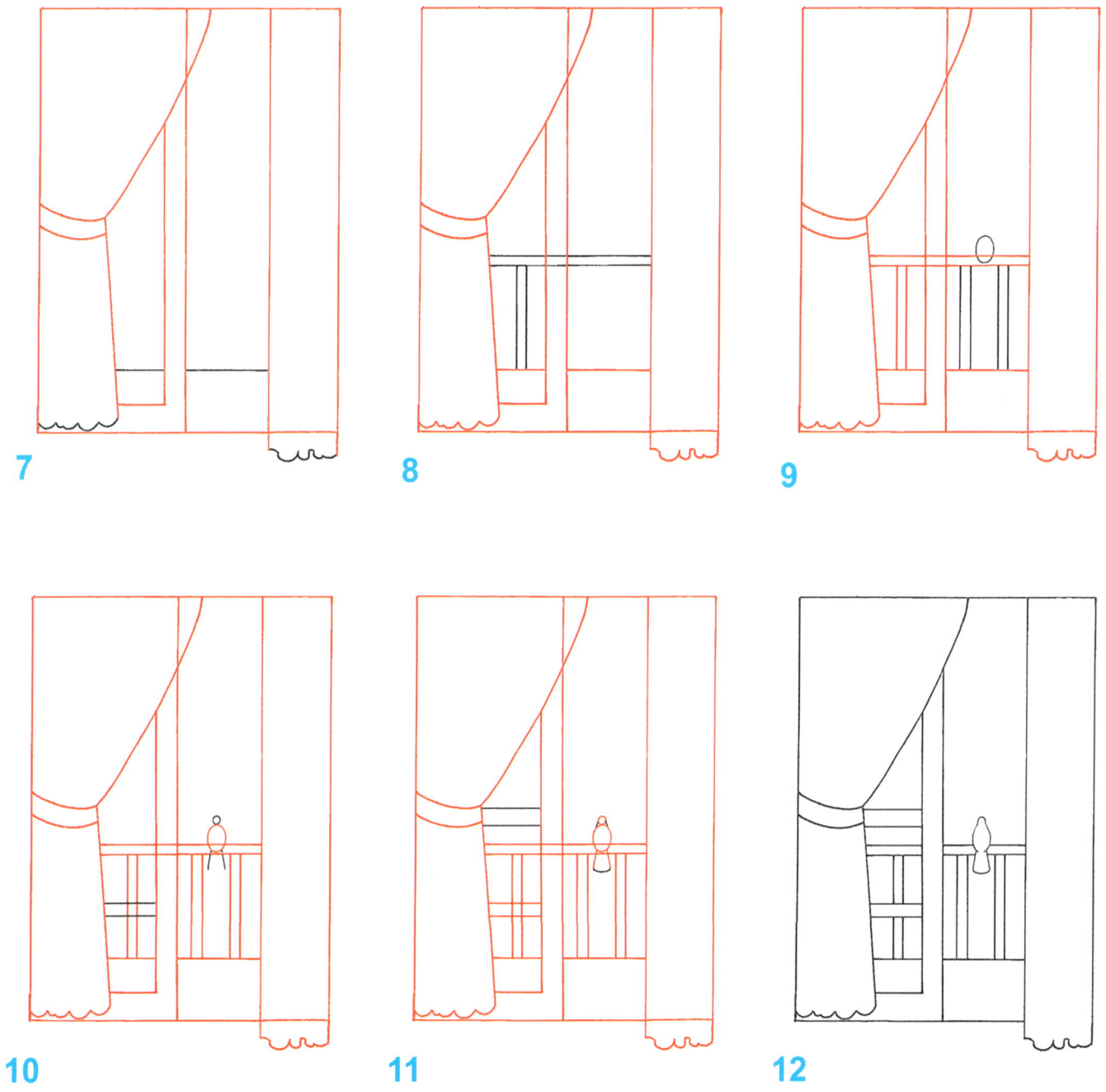

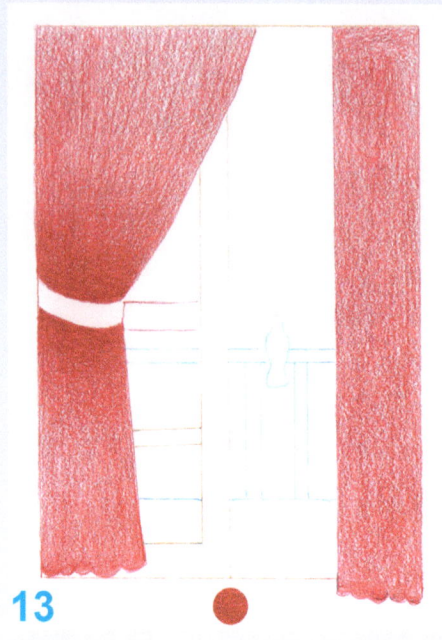
13 ●

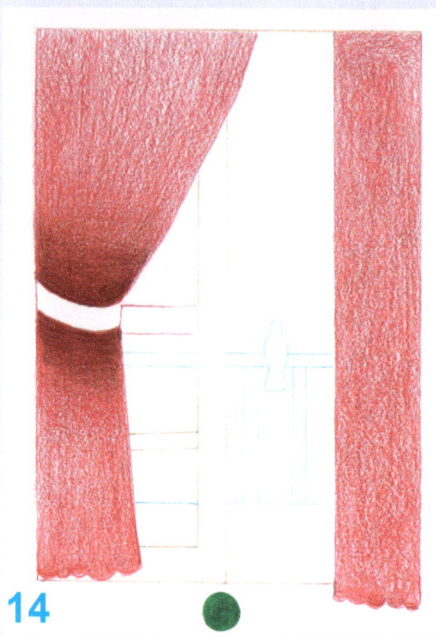
14 ●

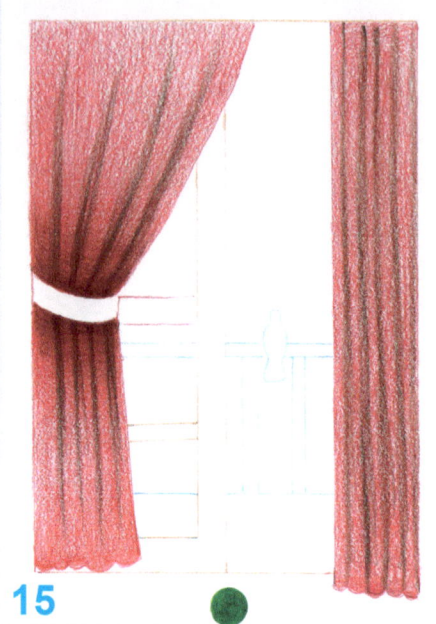
15 ●

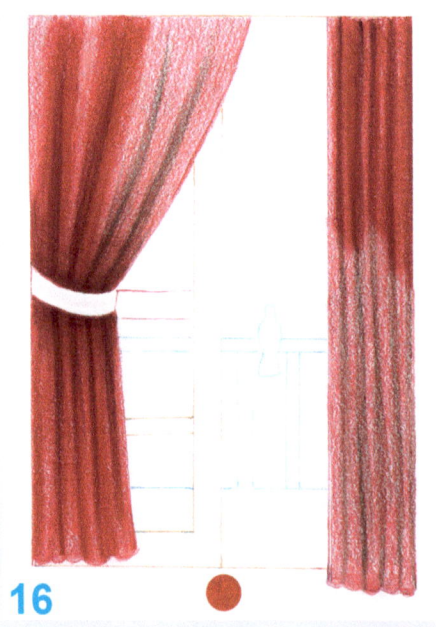
16 ●

17 ●
90

18 ●

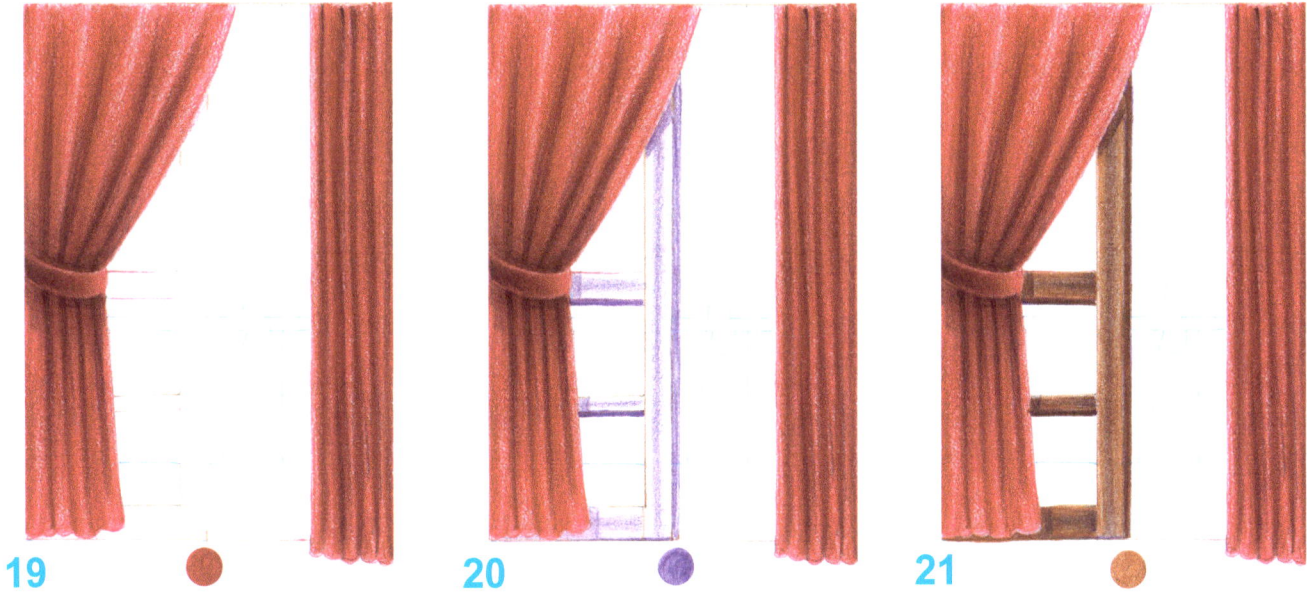

19 20 21

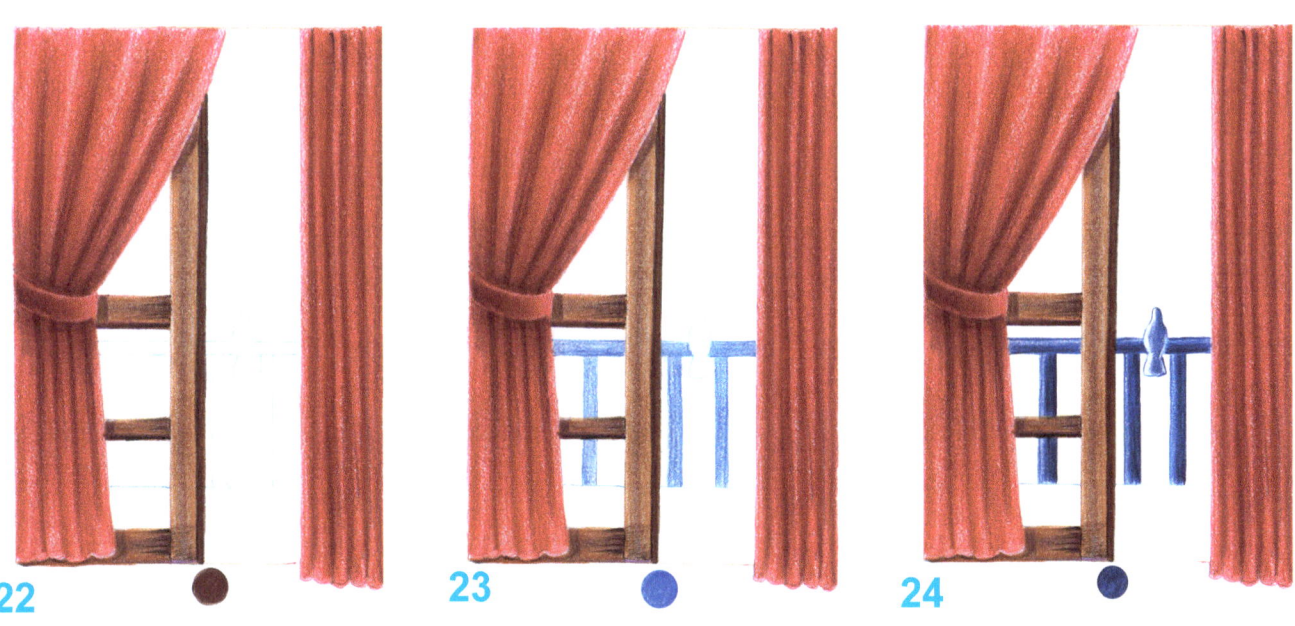

22 23 24

91

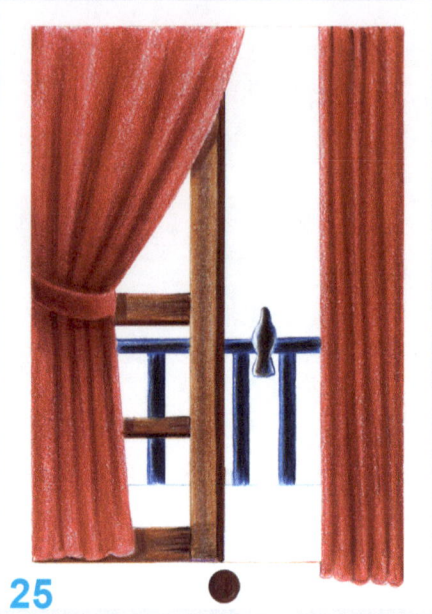
25 ●

26 ●

27 ●

28 ●

29 ●

92

30 ●

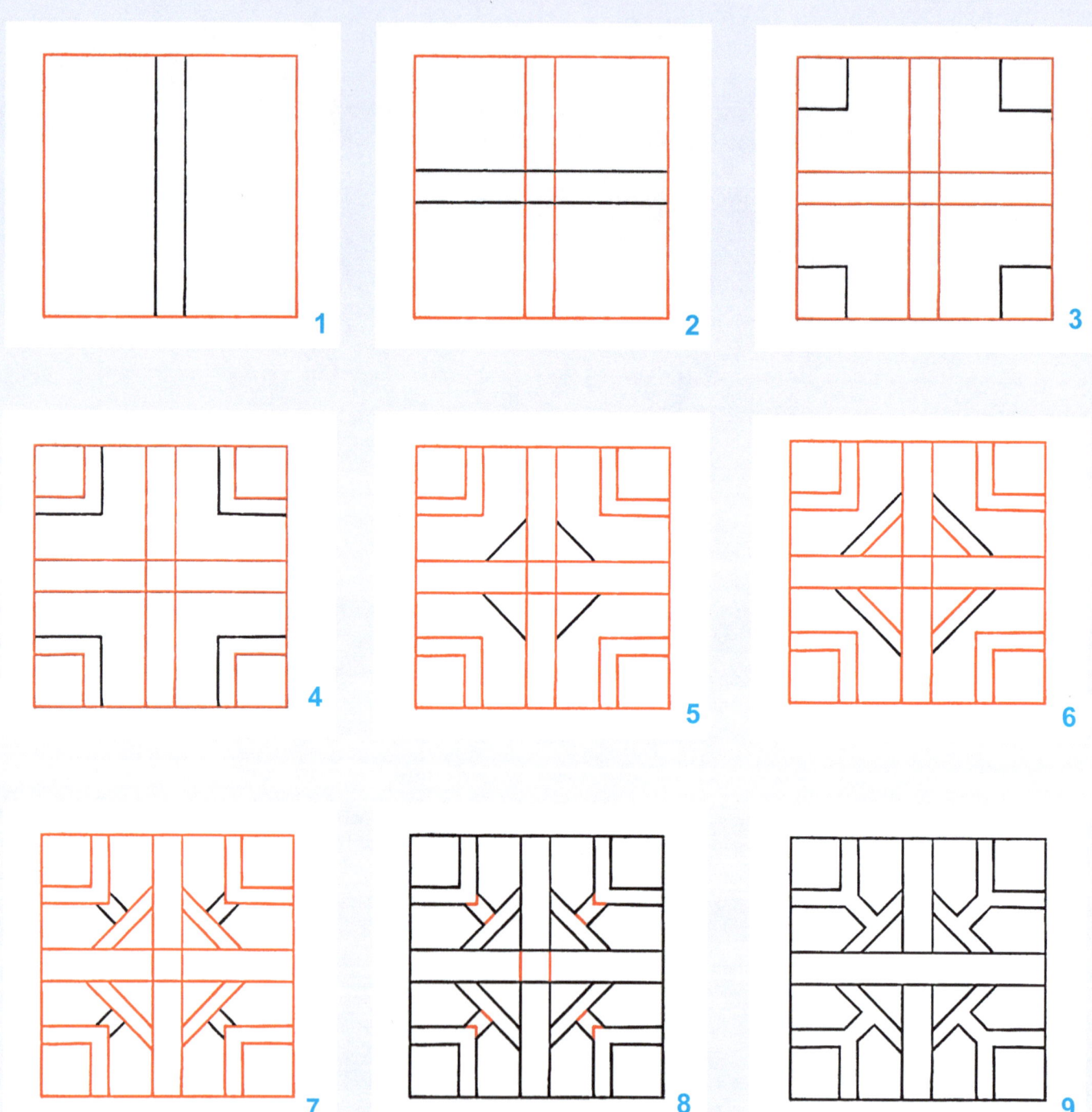

1

2

3

4

95

5 ● ● ●

6 ●

7 ● ●

8 ●

9 ●

10 ●

96

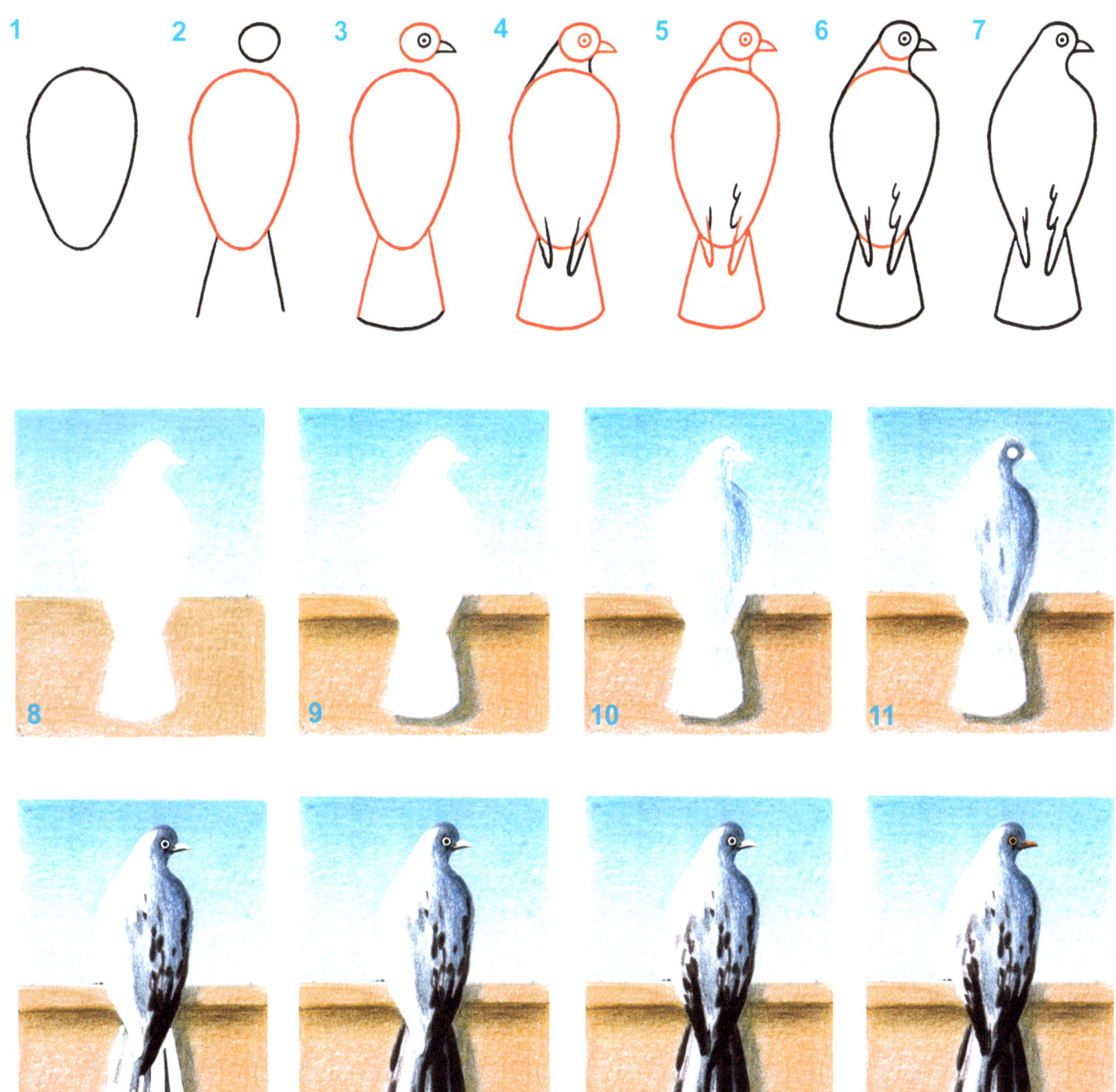

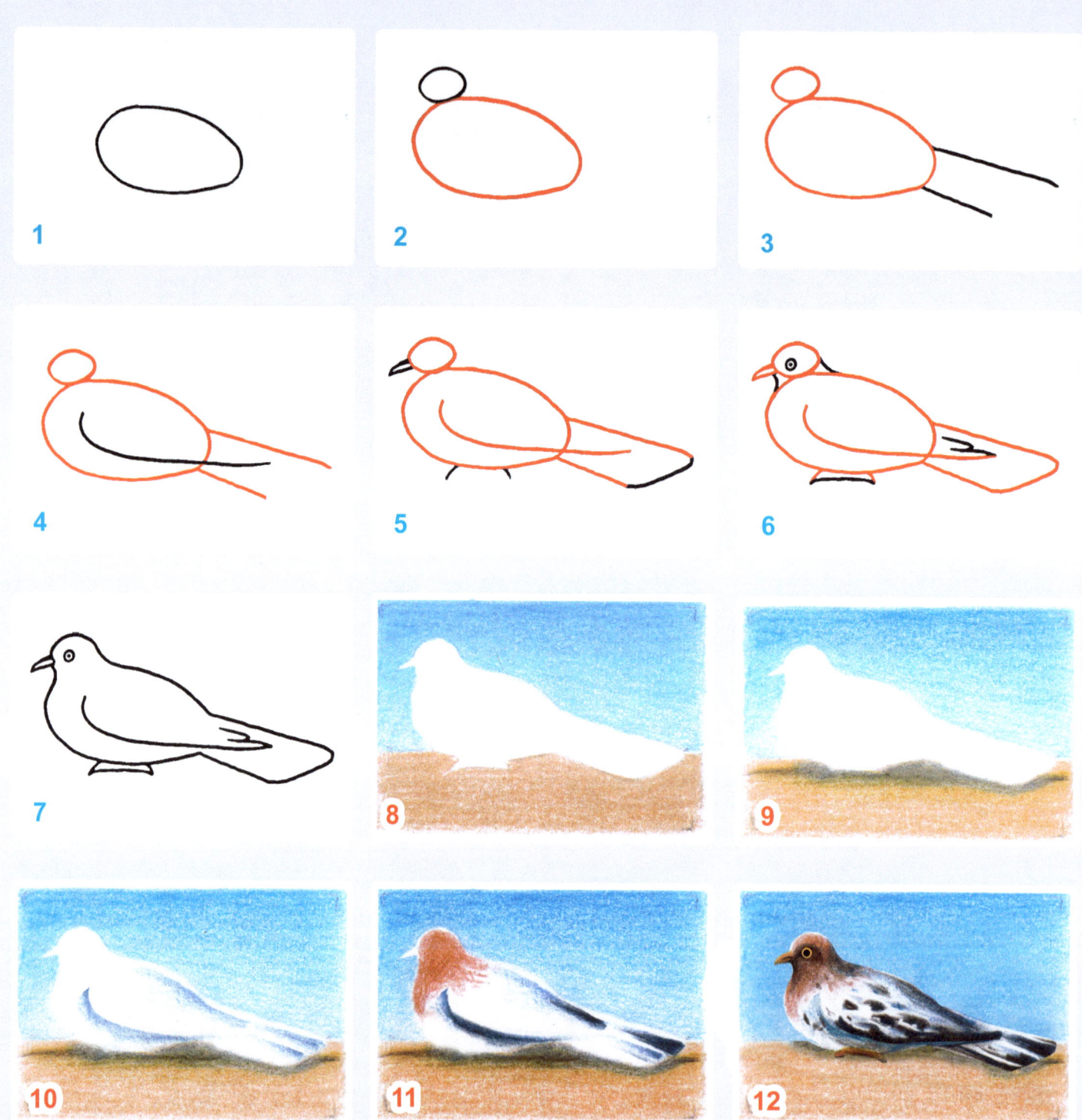

1

2

3

4

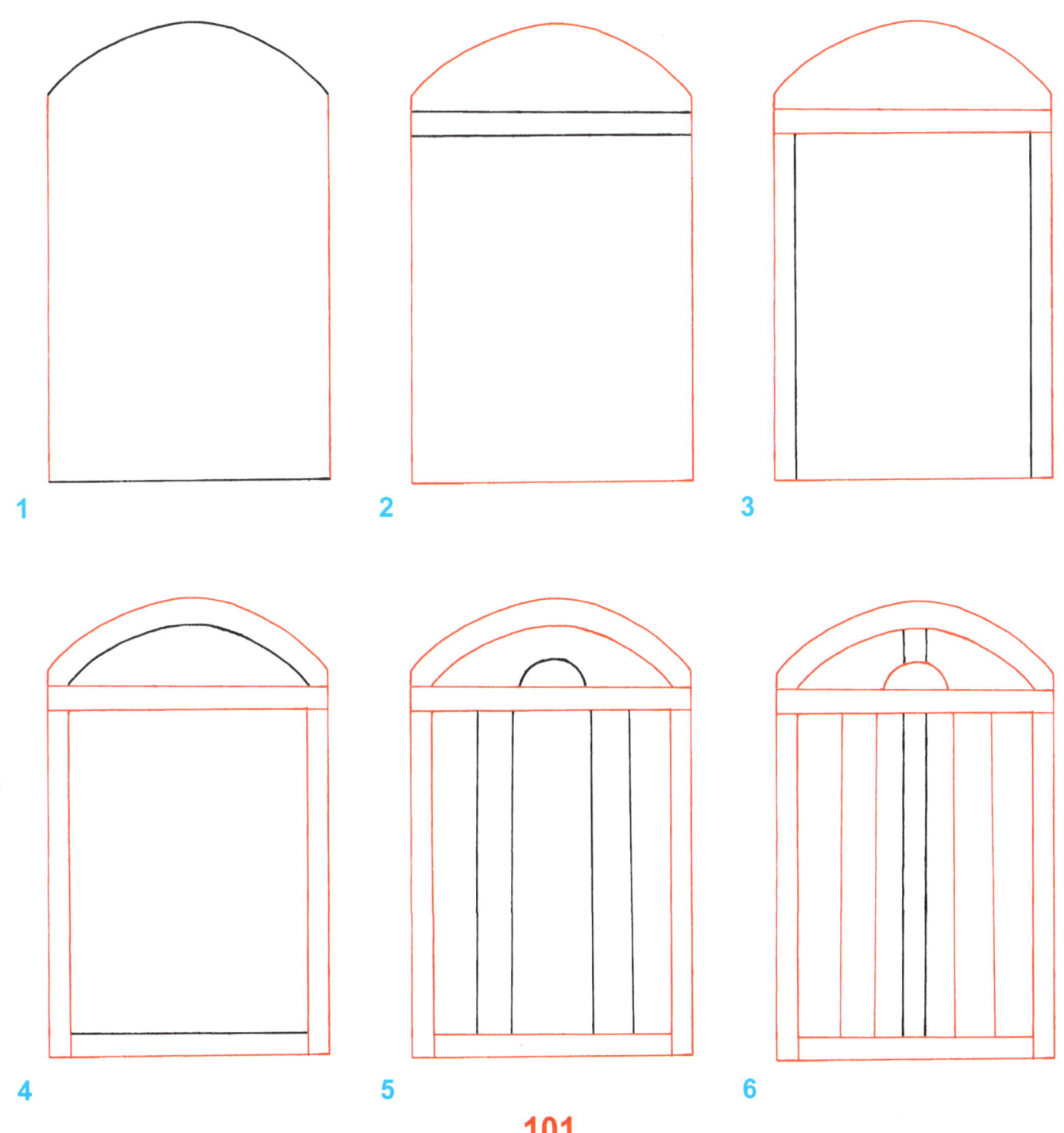

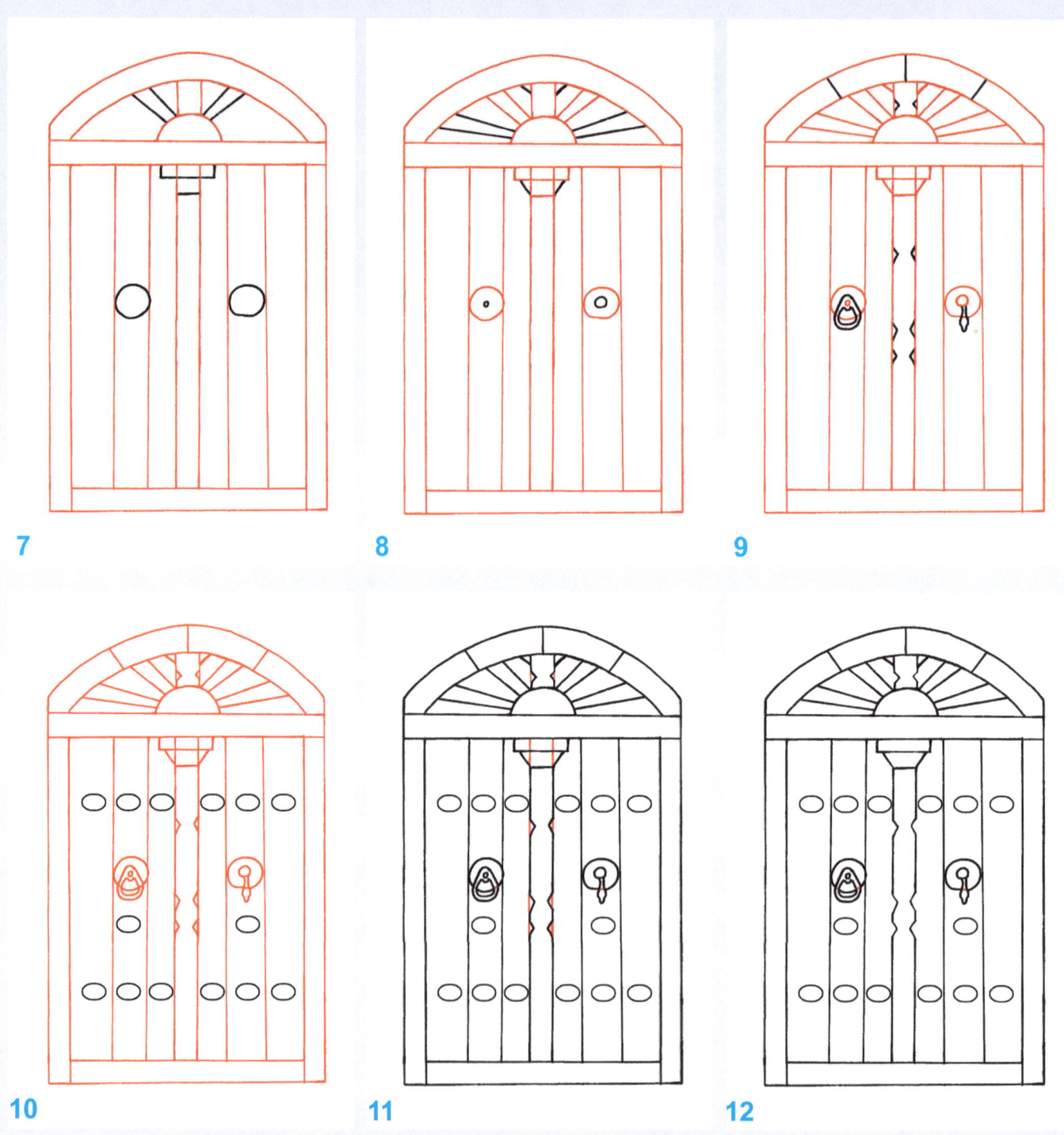

19

20

21

22

23

24

25 26 27

28 29 30

105

Mohammed Manochehri
Master of Visual Arts, Art teacher, the author of Sana Art Training Books in drawing, painting, collage, calligraphy.

Mohammad Manoochehri was born in Nowkandeh, a small town locate in the North of Iran, in an average family. He finished elementary and guidance school in Nowkandeh and graduated from high school in Bandargaz. In 2001, he took the degree of Associate of Arts in Visual Arts. Meanwhile, he ranked First in National Students Competition in drawing. Two years later, he returned to Tehran to continue studying in M.A. of visual Arts. After taking his M.A. degree, he returned to his hometown to teach at schools and Vocational schools. In 2006, he published his first Art Training book in drawing and painting. So far, he has published more than ten books in different fields of art such as drawing, painting, collage, calligraphy, and handwriting. In 2004, he published the present book in eight modern languages.

Author's forward

The ability to do something fast and carefully is called skill while art is creativity and innovation in every skill which is in the path of perfection! Therefore, the prerequisite and prior condition of art is being skillful. To motivate our children and beginners to show creativity and innovation, the new generation should be taught some special skills . In Sana series we have tried to make learning drawing , painting , and similar skills easy through applying mathematical simplification .

Sana Books Series and the applied method are the result of 30-year creative experience of the author who has not plagiarized from any sources. In fact, they are based on the author's experimental and individual thought which have been systematically presented .

In addition to teaching Art to children and adolescents using simplification (the same one used in mathematics), Sana book series seriously focuses on motivation and other goals, meaning improving general abilities in the new generation : Some of the general goals of Sana Art teaching are: internalizing mental and behavioral discipline along with improving concentration, self-confidence and self-esteem. Increasing positive imagination, improving the compatibility between mind and the hand, and boosting the threshold of tolerance are the other goals of the series .

Art is the best method and tool to improve the general abilities and talents of children and adolescents. If it is applied consciously and wisely, it will have marvelous results. Drawing and painting, because of paying step by step attention to the process , would improve the general abilities in children .

The steps in painting and drawing : 1 - observing   2 - memorizing   3 - depicting

1 - observing : As the required observation in drawing is accompanied with precision and a high level of concentration, it is per se an efficient exercise to increase precision and concentration in children .

2 - memorizing : Due to the improvement of conscious imagination in the second step (memorizing) , the ability of memorizing in children is naturally improved. It means the brain is getting sharper in learning .

3 - depicting : In the third step, drawing and painting (depicting) cause an intimate relationship between the brain and hand, leading into the ability to create handicrafts in children .

Relying on experiences and effectively, it has been consciously and wisely attempted to observe the following issues in Sana Training books .

In Sana book series of teaching Art, we follow the goals according to the interest and willingness in children and adolescents . We hope the desired improvement and development can help all the children from various ethnicities and nationalities to reach the top of salvation and redemption .

After acknowledging the positive and helpful effects of Sana Books , we hope you are motivated to provide the other books of the series so that the educational plans will be more effectively achieved in your dear children .

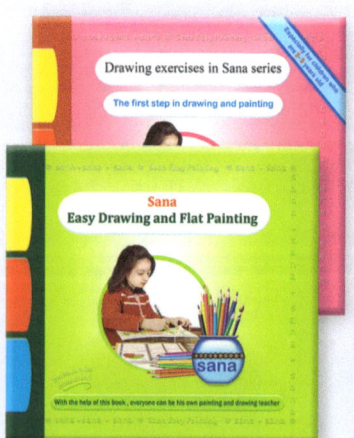
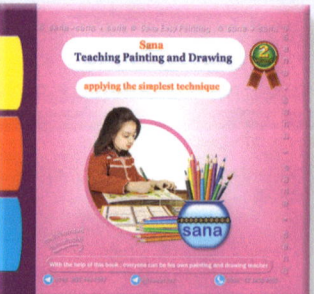
The other works published by the author ("Sana"Art Training Books)
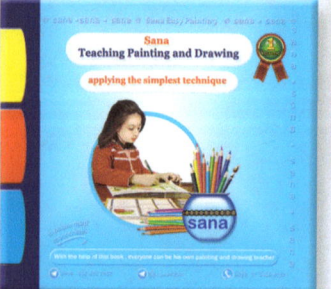
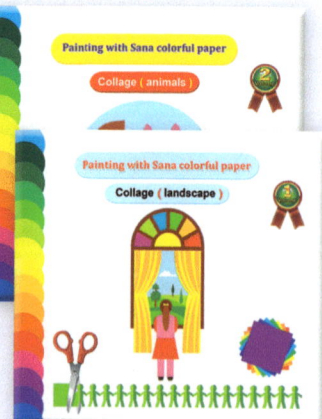

www.ingramcontent.com/pod-product-compliance
Lightning Source LLC
Chambersburg PA
CBHW042016150426
43197CB00002B/47